JAZZ RHYTHM GUITAR
THE COMPLETE GUIDE

ABOUT THE AUTHOR

Award winning guitarist Jack Grassel enjoyed years of personal tutorage by his mentors, Tal Farlow and George Van Eps, which helped father his unique style. In the March 2000 issue of *Guitar One* magazine, fans voted him as one of the "10 Best Guitarists (you probably don't know) in America," and stated "…he doesn't sound like any other guitar player." This winner of five WAMI awards as Jazz Artist of the Year maintains a busy schedule of performances. For decades, guitarists the world over have studied his many books and recordings. In 1996, Jack was acknowledged for excellence as a distinguished educator in "Who's Who of America's Teachers." Mr. Grassel's popular Big Ax book series is the groundbreaking system for playing bass lines, melody, and chords simultaneously, and his columns have enlightened readers of *Guitar Player* and *Just Jazz Guitar* magazines. Learn more about Jack and his work at www.jackgrassel.com.

ISBN 0-634-03275-5

7777 W. BLUEMOUND RD. P.O. BOX 13819 MILWAUKEE, WI 53213

Copyright © 1988 by Jenson Publications
International Copyright Secured   All Rights Reserved

No part of this publication may be reproduced in any form or by any means without the prior written permission of the Publisher.

Visit Hal Leonard Online at www.halleonard.com

TABLE OF CONTENTS

Introduction	3
The Function Of The Guitar In The Jazz Ensemble	4
Getting The Right Sound From The Guitar	5
Practice Techniques	7
Chord Construction and Notation	8
Two Forms of the Dominant Seventh	13
The Major and Minor Seventh	20
Chords with Alterations	25
Syncopated Latin Rhythms:	
The Samba and Bossa Nova Style	33
The Ninth Chord	38
Chords With Multiple Alterations	44
Eleventh and Suspended Fourth Chords	49
Sixth Chords	52
The Minor/Major Seventh Chord	56
The Thirteenth Chord	57
Diminished Chords	61
Bar Chords: Early Rock Rhythm Style	65
The "Power Chord": Heavy Metal Style	67
The "Chuck Berry" Early Rock Style	68
Sixteenth Note "Funk Rhythms"	70
Reggae	73
Triads with Altered Roots (Slash Chords)	74
Responding To Drum Fills, Horn Figures and Piano Players	75

INTRODUCTION

This book has been written in response to a demand for a fast, clear, modern method of teaching jazz ensemble performing skills to the guitarist.

This book will cover:

1. READING CHORD CHARTS
    - Learning to interpret the symbols that represent chords
    - Playing written rhythms correctly and coordinating them with the band

2. INCREASING CHORD VOCABULARY
    - Learning chords in all keys
    - Becoming familiar with the entire guitar neck
    - Learning how to play chords of all qualities and alterations in the correct style

To make your practice sessions fun, every example in the book is performed on the cassette tape. You can play along with the rhythm section and hear how the examples should sound.

The musicians on this recording are:
Jack Grassel, Guitar
Tom McGirr, Bass
Mike Lorenz, Drums

How to practice:

1. Listen to the example on tape while reading the music without playing.

2. At first, practice the example slowly without the tape and gradually speed up to the tape.

3. Play along with the tape.

4. Turn the balance control on your cassette player all the way to the right. This will take the guitar out of the mix and allow you to play with just bass and drums.

Don't forget to tune your guitar to the pitches on the tape.

Good luck and enjoy yourself!

THE FUNCTION OF THE GUITAR IN THE JAZZ ENSEMBLE

1. STYLE

   The guitar can add the color which makes many different styles of music sound just right. Whether it's Blues, Rock, Pop, Country-Western, Jazz or Reggae, the guitar sound changes to fit the style of music. The guitarist may use electronic sound altering devices, or different amp settings and pickups to change the color of the sound.

2. RHYTHM AND HARMONY

   One of the missions of the jazz ensemble guitarist should be to connect the rhythm section to the horns. When you play a chord with the winds, they will sound fuller and more in tune. When you play an accent or fill with the rhythm section, it will energize the whole band. So harmonically and rhythmically the guitar can be vital to the success of the jazz ensemble.

3. PLAYING LINES

   Very often in contemporary jazz ensemble writing the guitar will have a written line which is needed to make the chart work. It may be a melody with the trumpets, saxes or trombones; or it could be a rhythmic motive on one note in a Funk or Rock chart. In any case, it is very important for the guitarist to be able to read single line melodies as well as chord charts.

4. SOLO

   When the guitarist is called on to improvise, it should be in the style of the composition. If it is a jazz tune, the guitar should have a mellow jazz tone and play jazz type lines. If it is a rock chart, the guitar should have a distorted sound and play licks in a rock style. Playing the wrong type of solo in a work really detracts from the impact of the ensemble and could change the entire concept of the piece.

GETTING THE RIGHT SOUND FROM THE GUITAR

There are basically four types of guitar sounds:

1. Clean, flat, natural sound using the neck pickup, striking the strings over that pickup for a mellow jazz sound.

2. Clean, flat sound with a chorus effect, using the neck pickup for a Pop or Latin sound.

3. Clean, treble sound with a slight distortion (using bridge or middle pickup position) for Pop, Blues, Funk, 50's Rock or Country -Western.

4. Dirty, distorted treble sound for Heavy Metal, Pop Rock.

Ways to alter your sound:

1. Select the pickup(s) to be used: neck, bridge, middle or any combination.

2. Change the tone settings on the amp: bass, treble, mid-range.

3. Use effects contained in amp or external pedals and boxes. Distortion, overdrive, reverb, delay, flange, chorus, phase and octaver are a few of the many possibilities.

4. Select the area to strike the string. Most people are content to pick in the same place all the time, however, many of the sounds may be enhanced by moving the right hand to different places. Mellow tone near the neck, sharper tone near the bridge.

Amp placement:

The best place to put your amp is on the floor. You won't hear as much string and pick noise as you would if the amp was elevated. Place the amp to your left so your body is between your guitar and the amp. This will shield the guitar so you get less feedback. Never put your amp in front of you.

BASIC SOUND CHART

All combinations of guitars, amps and people are different. This chart is just a starting point for you to begin to develop your own sounds.

MUSIC TYPE	PICKUP	AMP SETTINGS 1-10			EFFECTS	STRING AREA
JAZZ		BASS	MID	TREBLE		
swing	neck	4	4	4	none (clean sound)	near neck, above pickup
latin	neck	5	4	5	none or chorus	near neck, above pickup
fusion	middle position or middle pickup	4	6	6	chorus or slight overdrive	near neck, above pickup
ROCK		BASS	MID	TREBLE		
blues 50's rock C and W	middle (on 3 pickup guitars, use bridge and middle)	4	6	8	slight overdrive to simulate old tube amplifiers	bridge, or midway between bridge and neck
pop top 40	middle (on 3 pickup guitars, use bridge and middle)	4	6	8	slight overdrive and/or chorus or whatever other effect is needed to duplicate the recording	bridge, or midway between bridge and neck
funk reggae	middle (on 3 pickup guitars, use bridge and middle)	4	4	8	wa wa pedal or phaser with rate set to simulate wa wa pedal	bridge, or midway between bridge and neck
heavy metal	bridge	4	6	10	distortion overdrive	above bridge pickup

PRACTICE TECHNIQUES

In order to improve steadily on an instrument, you should develop an efficient and organized practice schedule. These ideas will help you get the most out of your practice time.

1. THE PRACTICE AREA

    Have a practice area in your home away from distractions. It should be physically comfortable and well lit. You should have all your tools there: instrument, amp, music stand, metronome, music, staff paper, recordings to listen to and something to play them on, a comfortable chair without arms, a tape player to record yourself for self-analysis, and anything else that will help you practice better.

2. THE PRACTICE TIME

    Practice every day. If you miss one day, you will notice it. If you miss two or more days, your audience will notice it. It is better to practice 1/2 hour per day than two hours once a week. It is better to practice two separate 1/2 hour periods in one day than one hour once a day. The idea is to be productive the entire practice period. It's much easier to do this with several shorter periods rather than one long session.

3. THE PRACTICE MATERIALS

    It is helpful to make a list of the things you need to work on during your practice session. Alternate these materials during the practice period so you stay fresh and interested.

    Here's a sample list:

    A. Scales and technical exercises.

    B. Melodic and rhythmic chording.

    C. Work on soloing.

    D. Music reading: etudes and songs.

    E. Transcribing. Learn something by ear, and notate it on staff paper.

CHORD CONSTRUCTION AND NOTATION

All chords are constructed from scales. To make understanding chords easier, numbers are assigned to each degree (each note) of the scale.

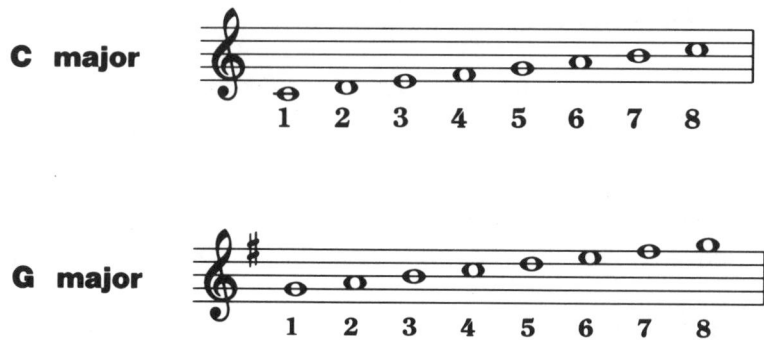

The root or "bass" note of each scale is given the number "1." All triads (three note chords) are built with 1 - 3 - 5.

Any extensions or alterations to the triad will be notated in the chord symbol. For example:

When the "MA7" was added, we added the seventh degree of the C major scale to the chord. Many other extensions and alterations are possible. Keep in mind the numbering system for each scale, and the main triad (1 -3 - 5) of each chord.

CHORD SYMBOLS

The symbols which represent chords have not yet been standardized, so there are different labels for chords that all mean the same thing. A guitar player should be familiar with all the labels so any music may be played. Memorize these symbols so you will be prepared when you come across them. All the notation applies to any chord, "C" is used as an example throughout.

1. THE TRIAD - Is it major, minor, diminished, or augmented?

    A. MAJOR - The C major triad may be notated in any of the following ways:

    B. MINOR - The minor triad has a lowered third. Instead of E as the third as in the major triad, the third in the minor chord is E flat. It can be notated as follows:

    C. DIMINISHED - Another three note chord is the C diminished chord. In addition to the lowered third, the fifth is also lowered. The C diminished triad would contain the pitches C, Eb, Gb.

    D. AUGMENTED - The last three note chord is augmented. This triad has a major third with the fifth raised a half step. It is spelled C, E, G#.

2. THE SEVENTH CHORD

A. MAJOR
To make a major seventh chord, the seventh degree of the scale is added to the basic triad.

B. DOMINANT
To make a C dominant seventh chord, lower the seventh a half step. This would be spelled C, E, G, Bb.

C. MINOR
The minor seventh chord has a lowered third and a lowered seventh. C minor seventh would be spelled: C, Eb, G, Bb.

D. MINOR-MAJOR
Another seventh is the minor-major seventh, using a minor triad with a major seventh on top.

E. HALF DIMINISHED
The half diminished seventh chord is the same as a minor seventh with a lowered fifth. It is spelled C, Eb, Gb, Bb.

F. DIMINISHED
The diminished seventh chord has a lowered third and fifth. The seventh is lowered twice. The C diminished triad would be spelled C, Eb, Gb, Bbb.

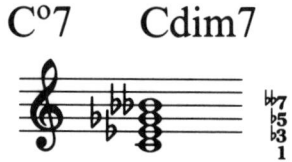

3. EXTENSIONS - These are the odd numbered scale degrees above the seventh: the ninth, eleventh and thirteenth.

    CMA9 means a CMA7 with a 9 on top.

All the different ways of writing the C major 7 also apply to the ninth.

    Cmaj9   CM9   Cma9

    C9 - (C ninth) means a dominant seventh with a 9 on top.
    Cmi9 - (C minor ninth) means a minor seventh with a 9 on top.

The eleventh chord contains the seventh and the ninth. The thirteenth chord contains the seventh, ninth and eleventh.

    Cmi11 - means Cmi7 with the 9 and 11 added.
    Cmi13 - means Cmi7 with the 9 and 11 and 13 added.

If there is nothing before the number of the type of chord, the chord is dominant: a major triad with the lowered seventh added.

    C9 - means a C7 with an added ninth.
    C11 - means a C7 with an added ninth and eleventh.
    C13 - means a C7 with an added ninth, eleventh, and thirteenth.

4. ALTERATIONS - This part of the label tells if a certain note (or notes) is raised or lowered 1/2 step (1 fret). The notes which are altered are usually the 5, 9, 11 or 13. The alteration is the last part of the label. Study the example on the next page to review chord symbol notation using extensions and alterations.

    There are three things that are shown in a chord symbol:

    a. The root of the chord.

    b. The quality of the chord. (Could be major, minor, augmented or diminished.)

    c. Extensions and alterations of the chord. (Is there a raised fifth or eleventh? Is there a raised or lowered ninth?)

The (#9) means the ninth of the chord is raised one half-step from the ninth of the major scale.

The root of this chord is C.

C7(#5#9)
C7+5+9
C+7(#9)

The "+" is an alteration. The fifth degree has been raised one half step.

The "7" means the chord contains 1-3-5-7. If the seventh does not say "MA," it should be lowered a half step from the major scale.

The name of this chord is "C seven sharp nine with a raised fifth."

It is spelled: C E G# Bb D#

5. ADDITIONS - It is taken for granted that if a thirteenth chord is notated, it should also contain the eleventh and ninth as well as the basic seventh chord. In some cases, the thirteenth might be needed without the eleventh. This chord would be labeled:

 D9 (add 13) or D13 (no 11)

The suspended chord is often used. This chord has a fourth instead of a third, with a minor seventh.

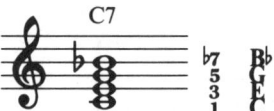   

Sometimes you will find C7 (no fifth). These kinds of chords are very awkward on the guitar. Locate the fifth (G) in the C7 chord and delete it. The easiest way to do this is to pluck the strings individually at the same time, (like a classical guitarist) and not strike the fifth.

Another kind of chord is a triad with an altered root or "slash chord." The note on the right of the slash is the note in the bass. If possible, you should play the bass note on the bottom of your chord. If it is not technically possible, just ignore the bass note and play the chord on the left of the slash.

Example: Dmi7/E

This will also work for polychords. A polychord is two triads stacked on each other.

Example: F
           ──
           Eb

The guitarist should play just the top triad in a high voicing with these chords.

TWO FORMS OF THE DOMINANT SEVENTH

3 X 2 4 1 X
CHORD
ROOT "C"
C#,Db
D
D#,Eb
E
F
F#,Gb
G
G#,Ab
A
A#,Bb

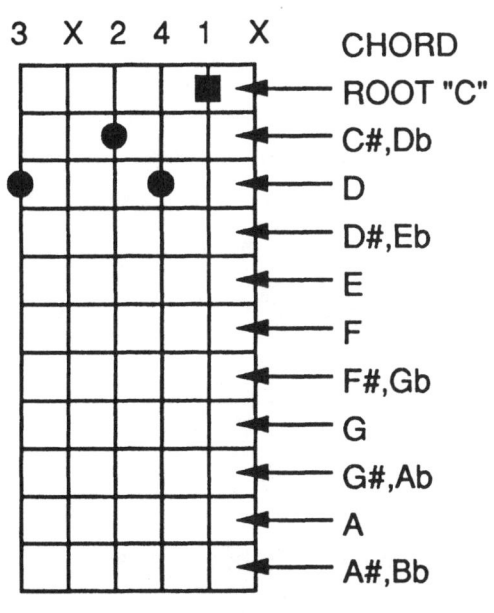

All the chord forms in this book will be based on two dominant seventh forms for simplicity and quick memorization. The first of these is the C7 form. It is C7 in the first fret, but changes as it is moved around the neck. The first and fifth strings are muted by touching parts of the fingers to those strings as they go past those strings on the way to their destinations.By using four note chords, there is a finger for each note so each note may be moved freely to change the chord to include the alterations and extensions which will come later in the book. The square on the diagram is the root of the chord. The name of the chord is the same as the name of the note played in that position. The style of strumming in the next few examples is the "Freddie Greene-Count Basie straight ahead" jazz style. Accent the second and fourth beats, use the neck pickup and strum lightly near the neck over the pickup. The number above the chord in the example is the fret in which the lowest chord note is played. In this style, the pressure of the left hand is released after each strum. Listen to the tape.

Ex. 1

Medium Swing

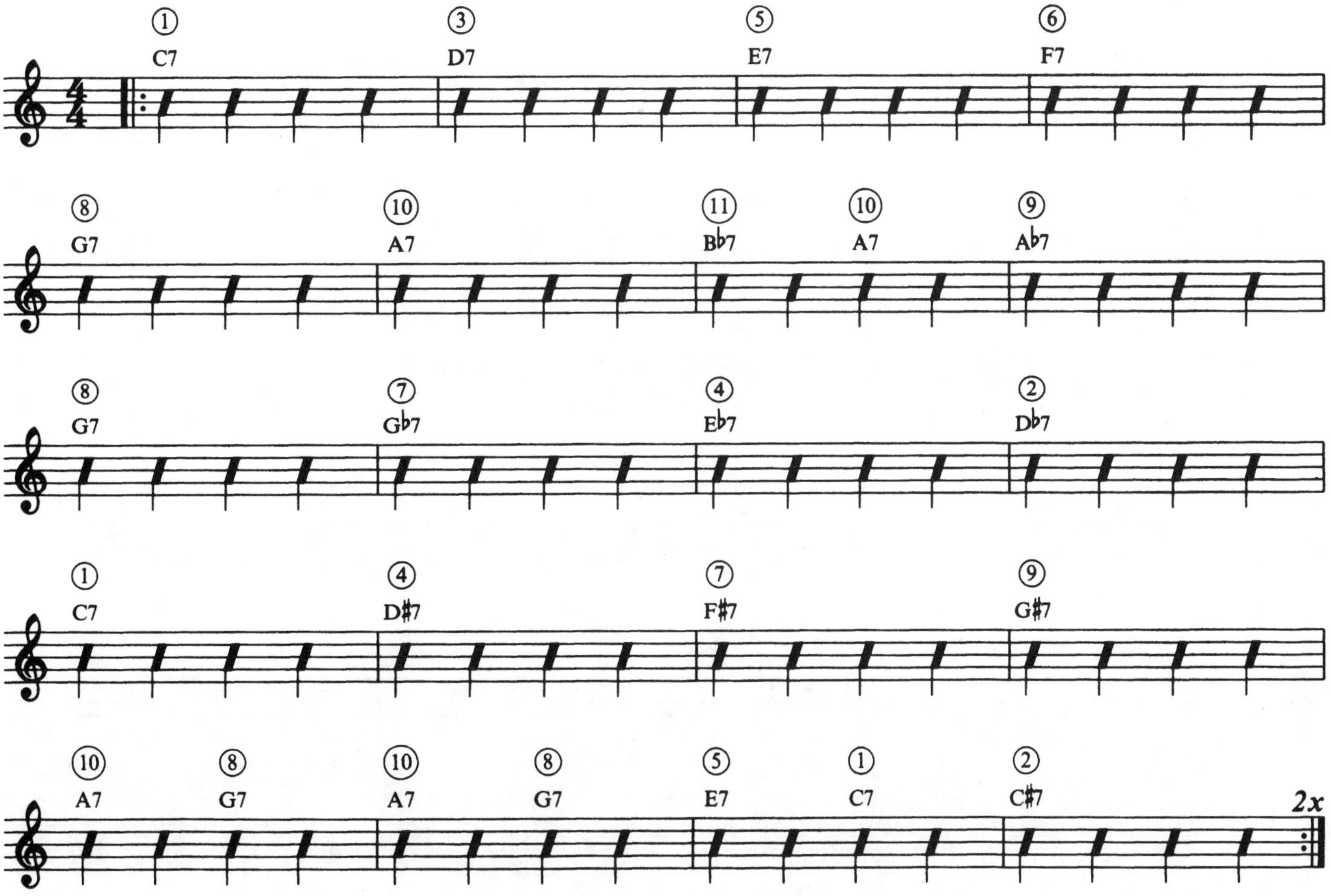

① C7
③ D7
⑤ E7
⑥ F7
⑧ G7
⑩ A7
⑪ B♭7
⑩ A7
⑨ A♭7
⑧ G7
⑦ G♭7
④ E♭7
② D♭7
① C7
④ D♯7
⑦ F♯7
⑨ G♯7
⑩ A7
⑧ G7
⑩ A7
⑧ G7
⑤ E7
① C7
② C♯7
2x

RHYTHM STUDIES

Using the C7 form, the following study incorporates rests, and different chord lengths which are multiples of the single quarter note rhythm of the previous page.

1. RESTS

QUARTER REST	𝄽	1 beat
HALF REST	▬	2 beats
WHOLE REST	▬	4 beats

2. NOTES

QUARTER NOTE	♩	1 beat
HALF NOTE	♩	2 beats
DOTTED HALF NOTE	♩·	3 beats
WHOLE NOTE	𝅝	4 beats

Remember to stop the string so nothing is heard during the rests. Either release the pressure with the left hand, or mute all 6 strings with right palm.

Ex. 2

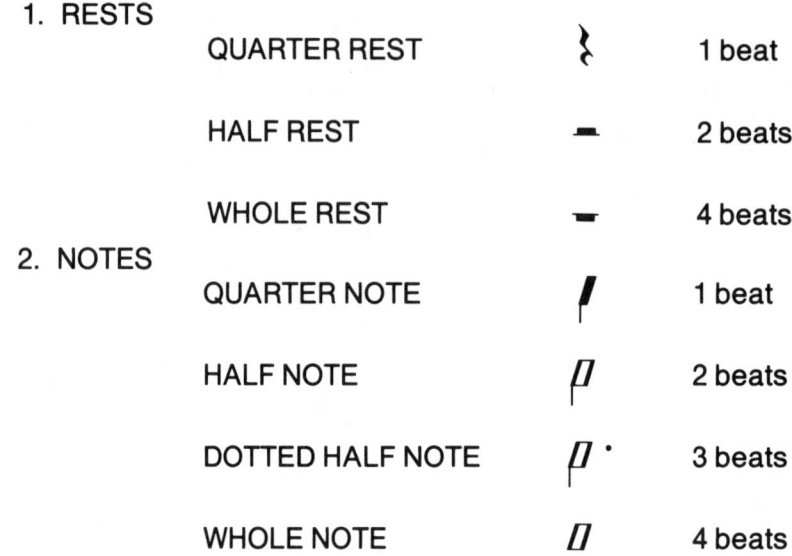

14

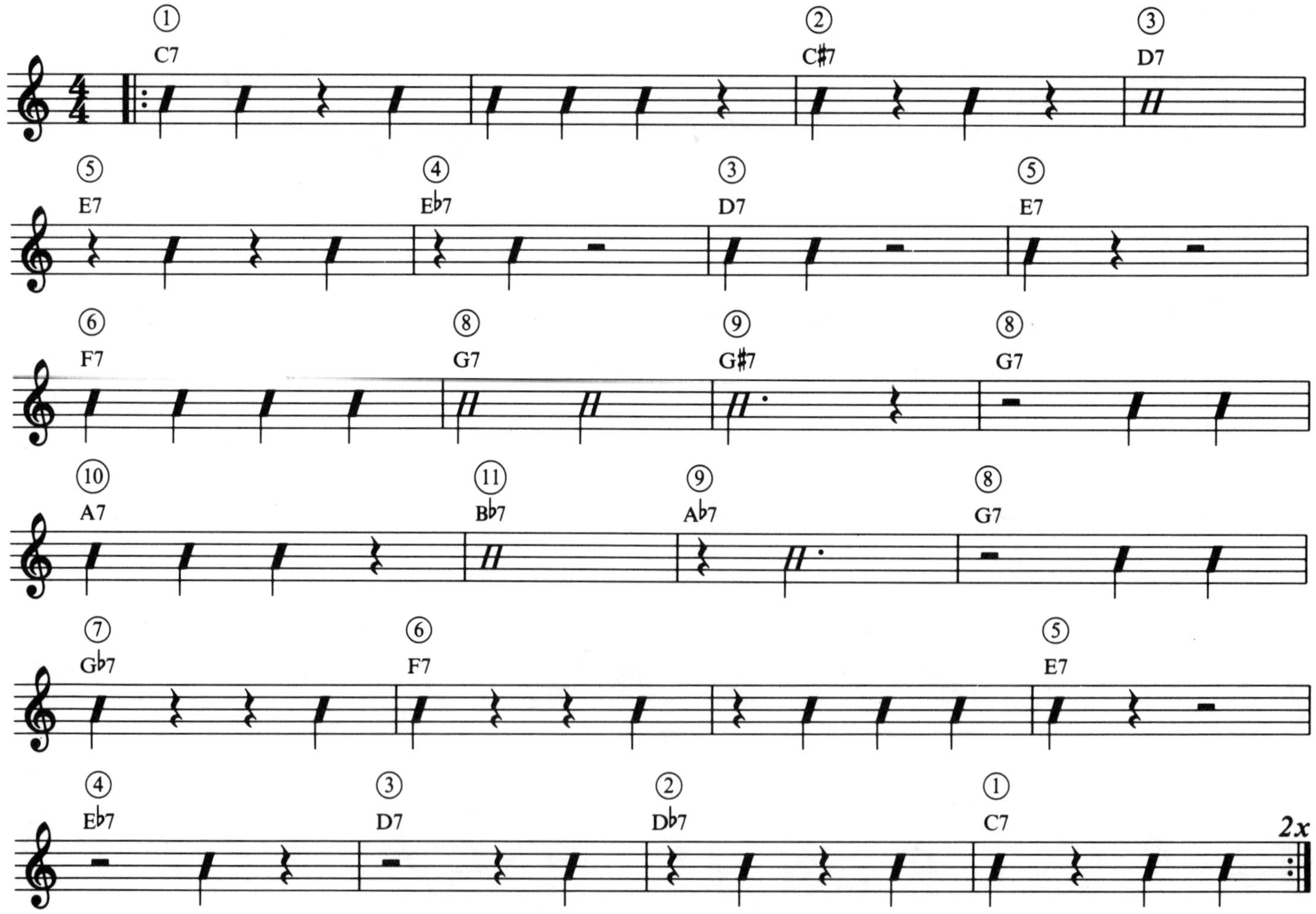

THE G7 FORM

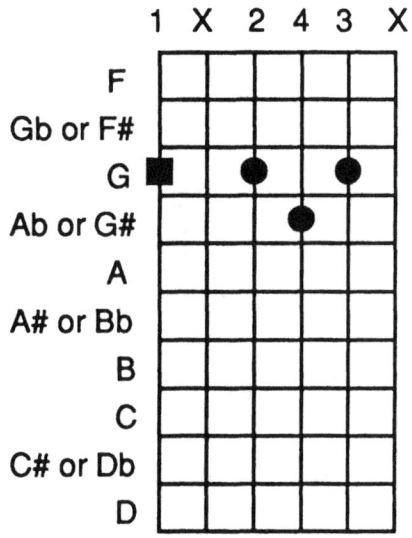

The root of this chord is on the sixth string. The first and fifth strings are muted by the fingers of the left hand. The 5th string is muted by the side of the first finger. The first string is muted by the side of the fourth finger. This example is still in the "Count Basie" jazz style so remember to accent two and four and release the left hand after each strum. Don't lift your hand up, but just release the pressure and leave your fingers on the strings.

Ex. 3
Swing

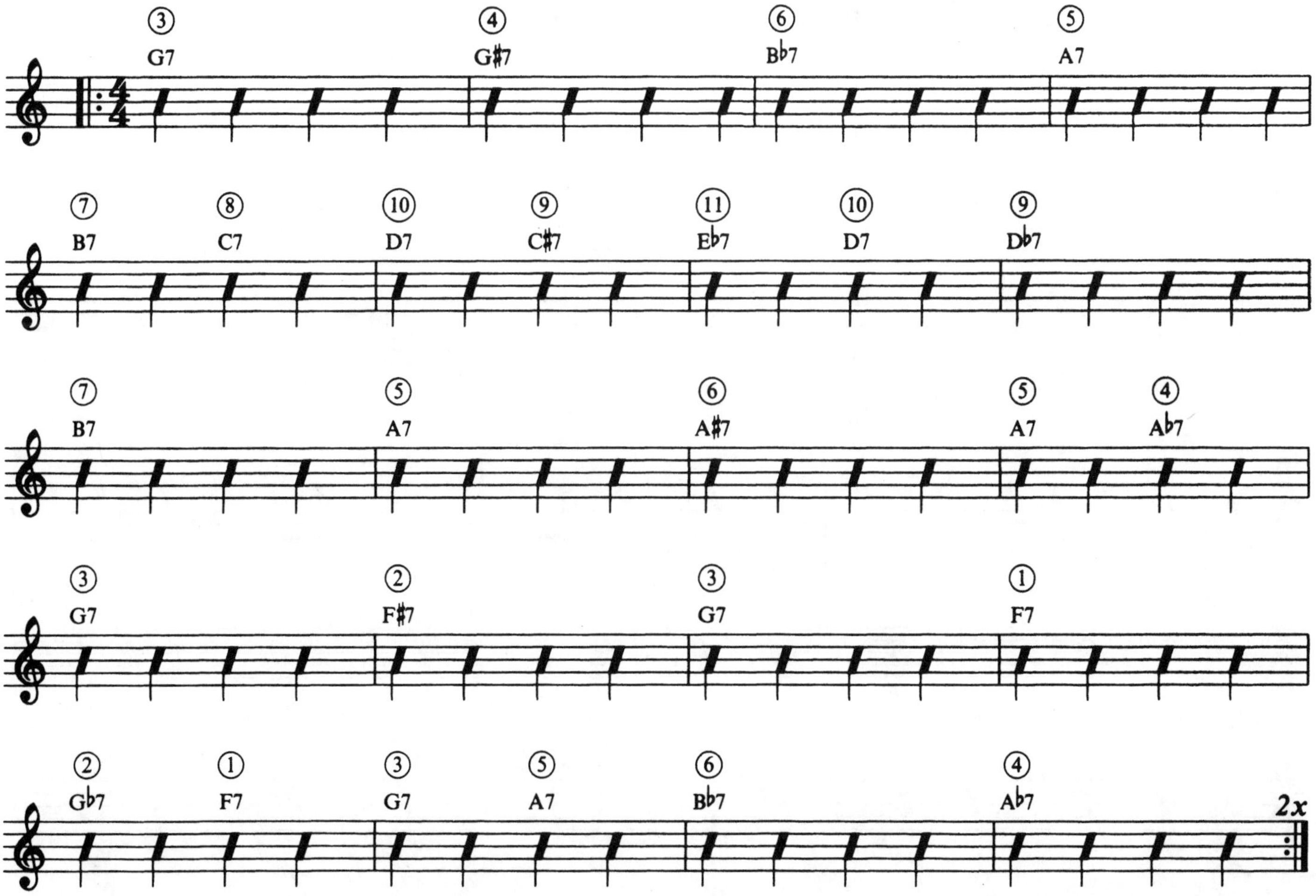

RHYTHM STUDIES

Ex. 4 Use the G7 form:

Swing

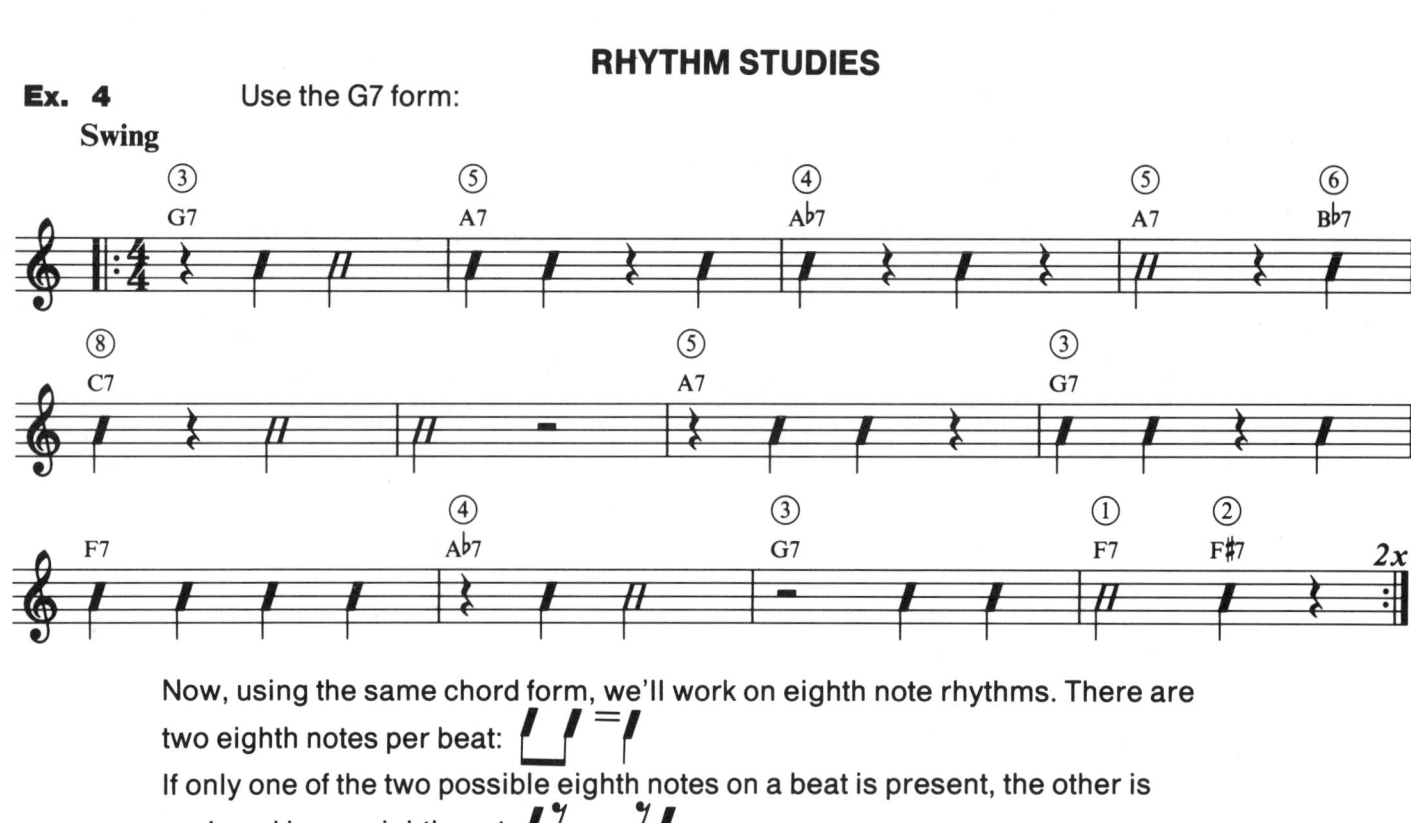

Now, using the same chord form, we'll work on eighth note rhythms. There are two eighth notes per beat:

If only one of the two possible eighth notes on a beat is present, the other is replaced by an eighth rest: or

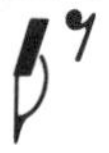

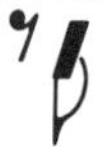

This is what it looks like when the chords are struck between the beats, or "on the and":

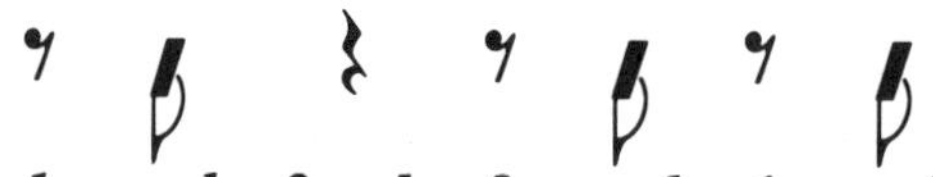

Count: 1 and 2and 3 and 4 and

Ex. 5 Remember to stop the chord so there is no sound during the rest.

Swing

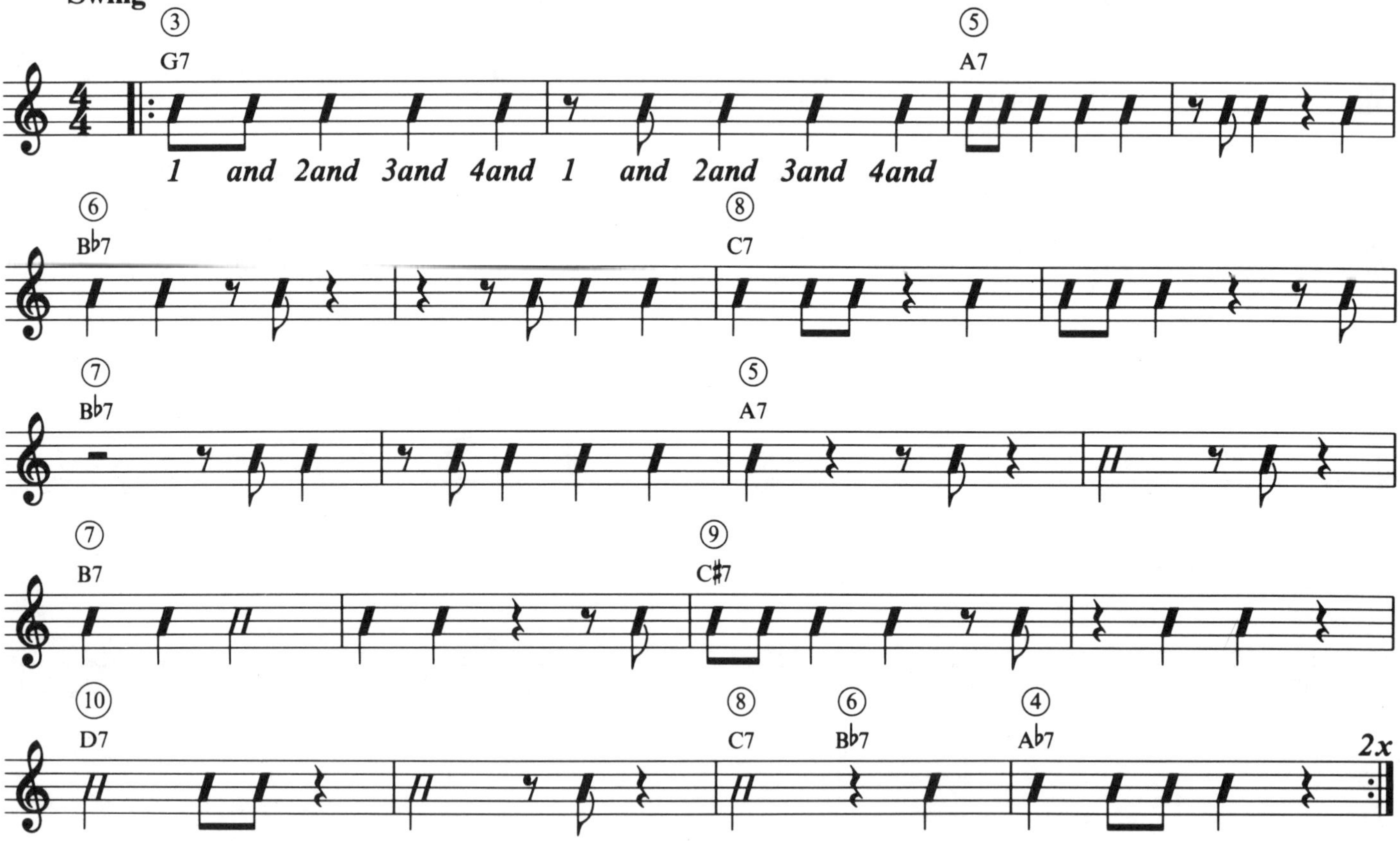

COMBINING THE TWO CHORD FORMS

A very common movement in music is the movement of the V (five chord, root on the fifth degree of the key) to the I (one chord, root on the first degree of the key). For example, in the key of C, the V chord is G. When going from the G7 chord to the C7 chord, a V-I progression is played.

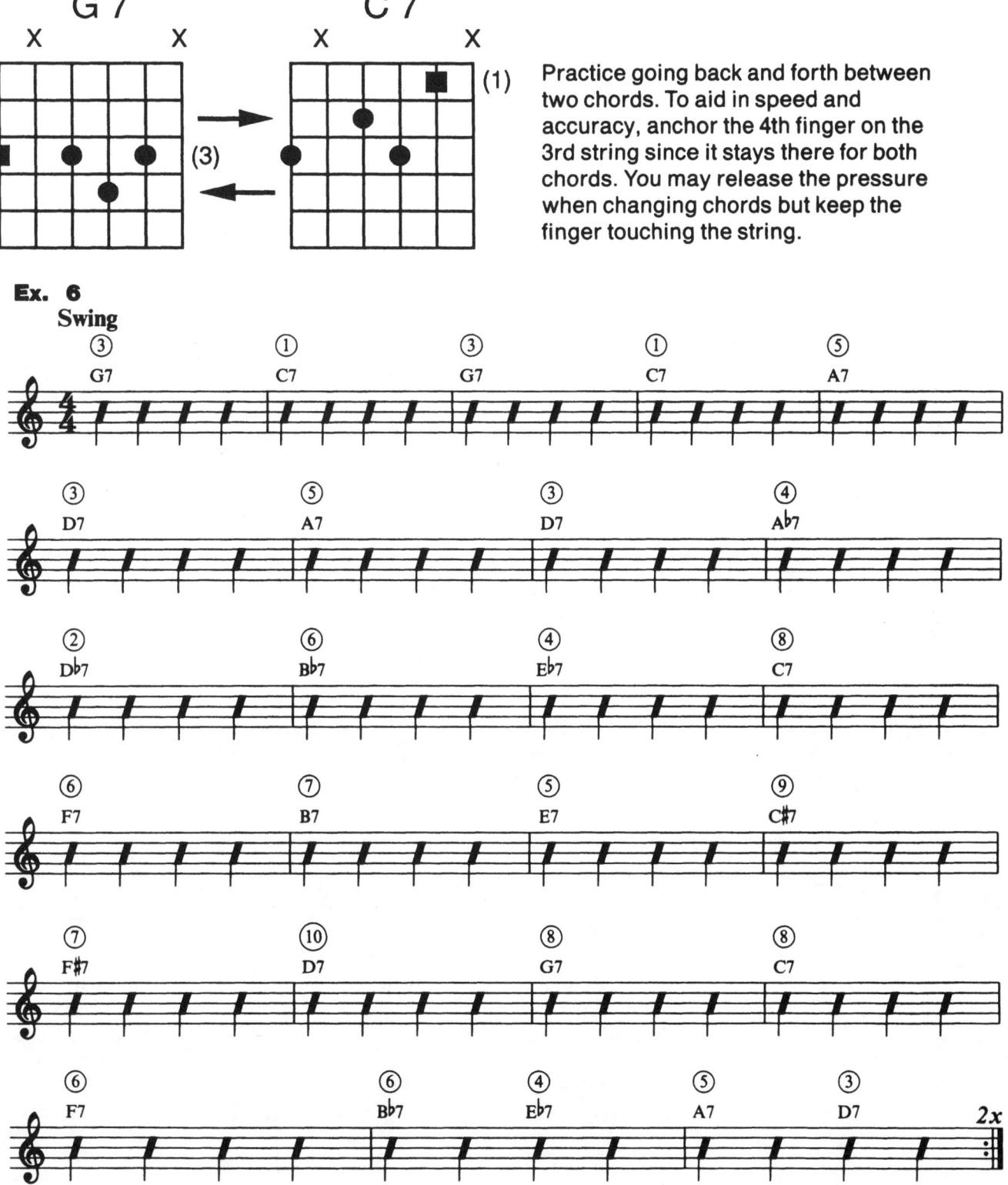

(1) Practice going back and forth between two chords. To aid in speed and accuracy, anchor the 4th finger on the 3rd string since it stays there for both chords. You may release the pressure when changing chords but keep the finger touching the string.

The movement of the previous page will now be played with the two chords reversing roles. The G7 chord will now act as the V chord resolving to the C7 form acting as the I chord. Note that the C7 form which is C7 in the first fret becomes G7 when played in the eighth fret. The G7 form which is G7 in the third fret becomes C7 in the eighth fret.

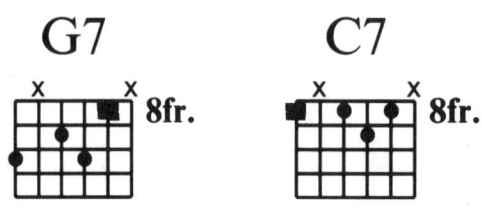

Ex. 7

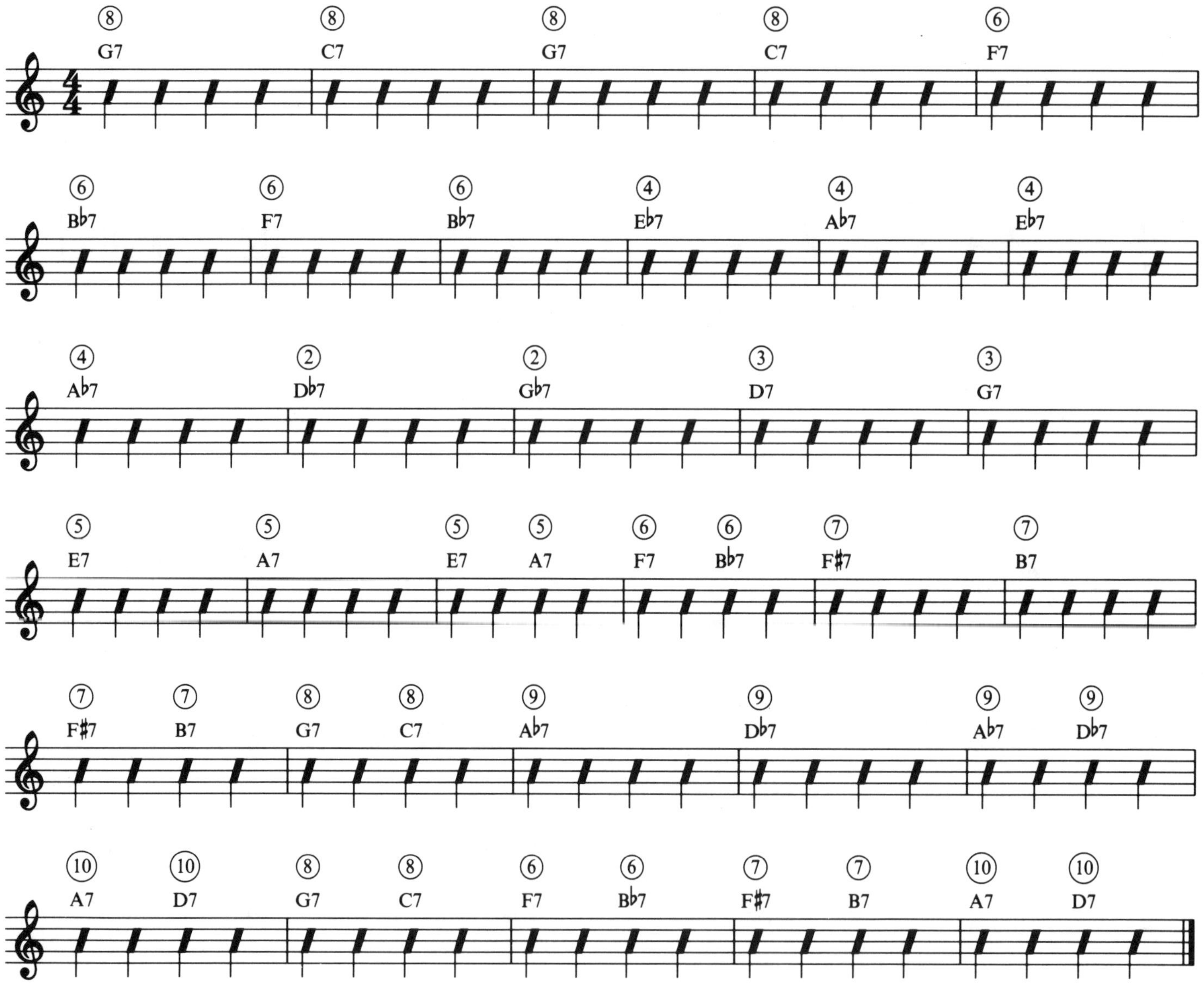

REVIEW

In this study, the two chords are placed over the neck at random. The fret number is given, however you must decide which of the two forms to use to achieve the desired chord.

Ex. 8

THE MAJOR AND MINOR SEVENTH

Using the two chord forms learned earlier as a base, the chord qualities will now be changed to include a minor seventh and a major seventh. Please review chord construction theory on page 9. The construction of a dominant seventh is 1, 3, 5, b7. The minor seventh structure will have a lowered third as well as a lowered seventh; 1, b3, 5, b7. The major seventh chord will use the four notes directly from the major scale; 1, 3, 5, 7. Before playing example 9, practice going back and forth from one form to another.

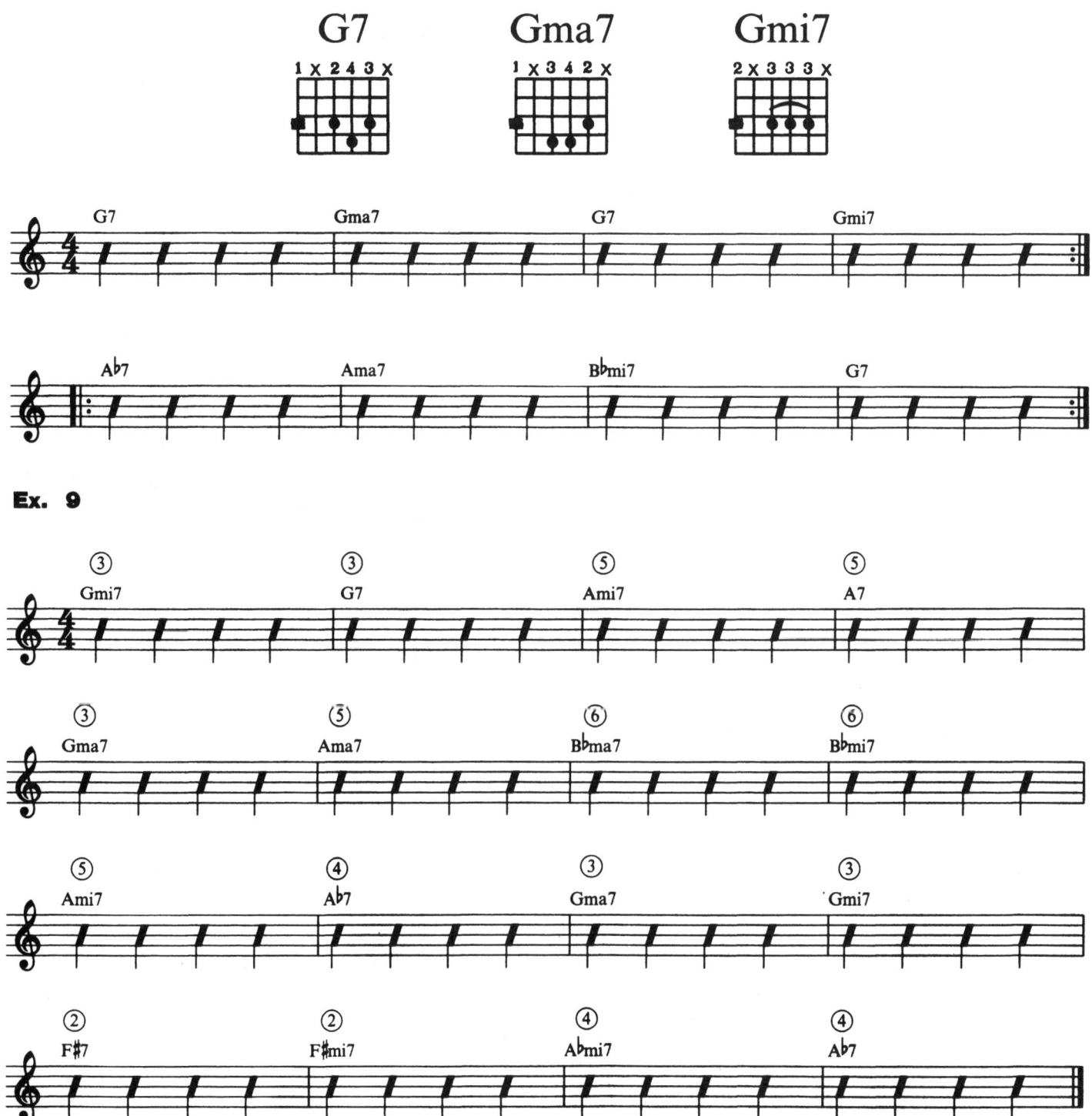

Ex. 9

STUDY GUIDE

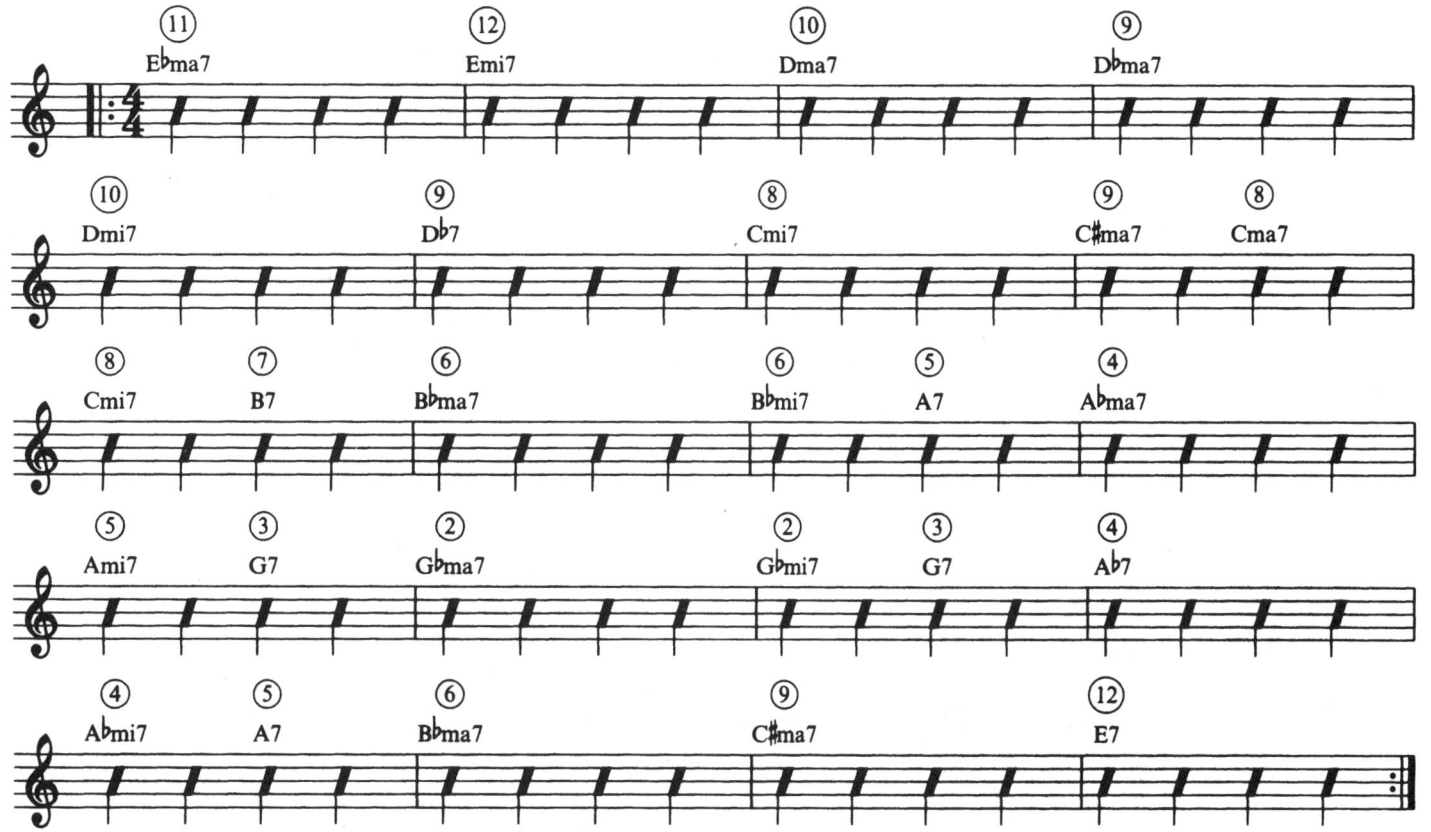

RHYTHM STUDY

Ex. 10

Using major, minor and dominant forms.

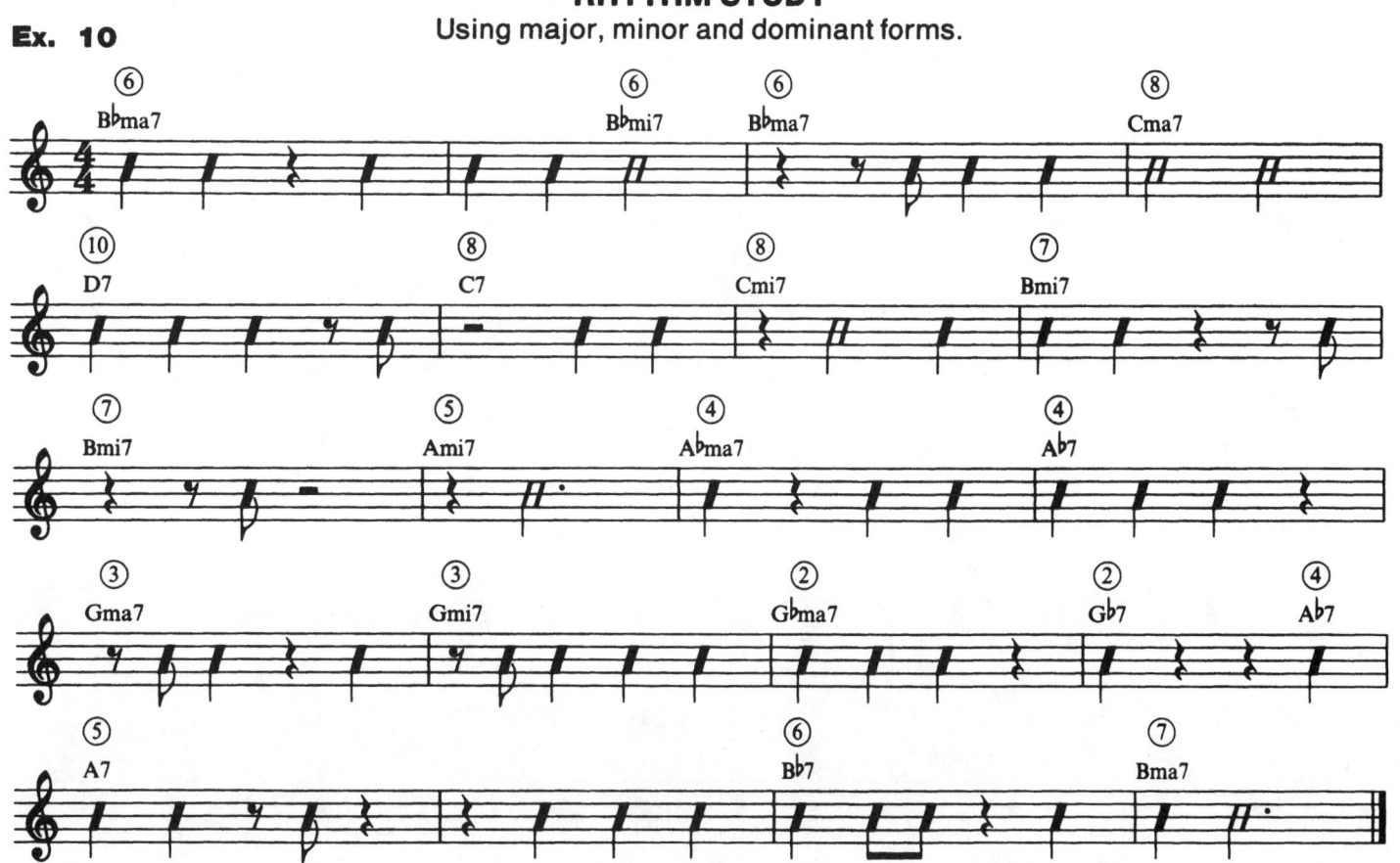

BUILDING MINOR AND MAJOR SEVENTHS ON THE C7 FORM

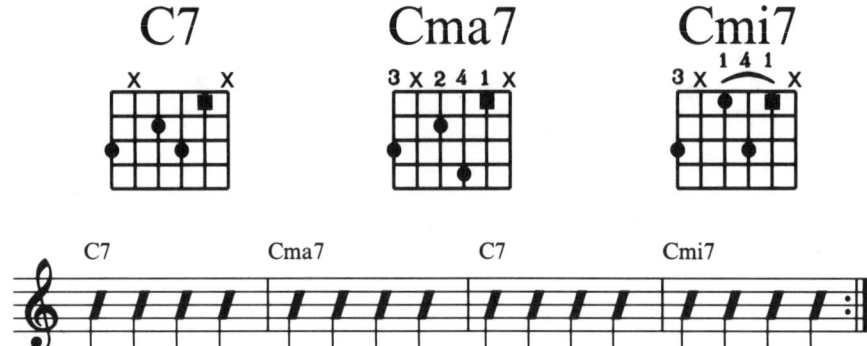

This major seventh voicing may sound strange by itself at first, but in an ensemble it sounds very good. This voicing is also very easy to get to from the dominant and minor seventh forms.

Ex. 11

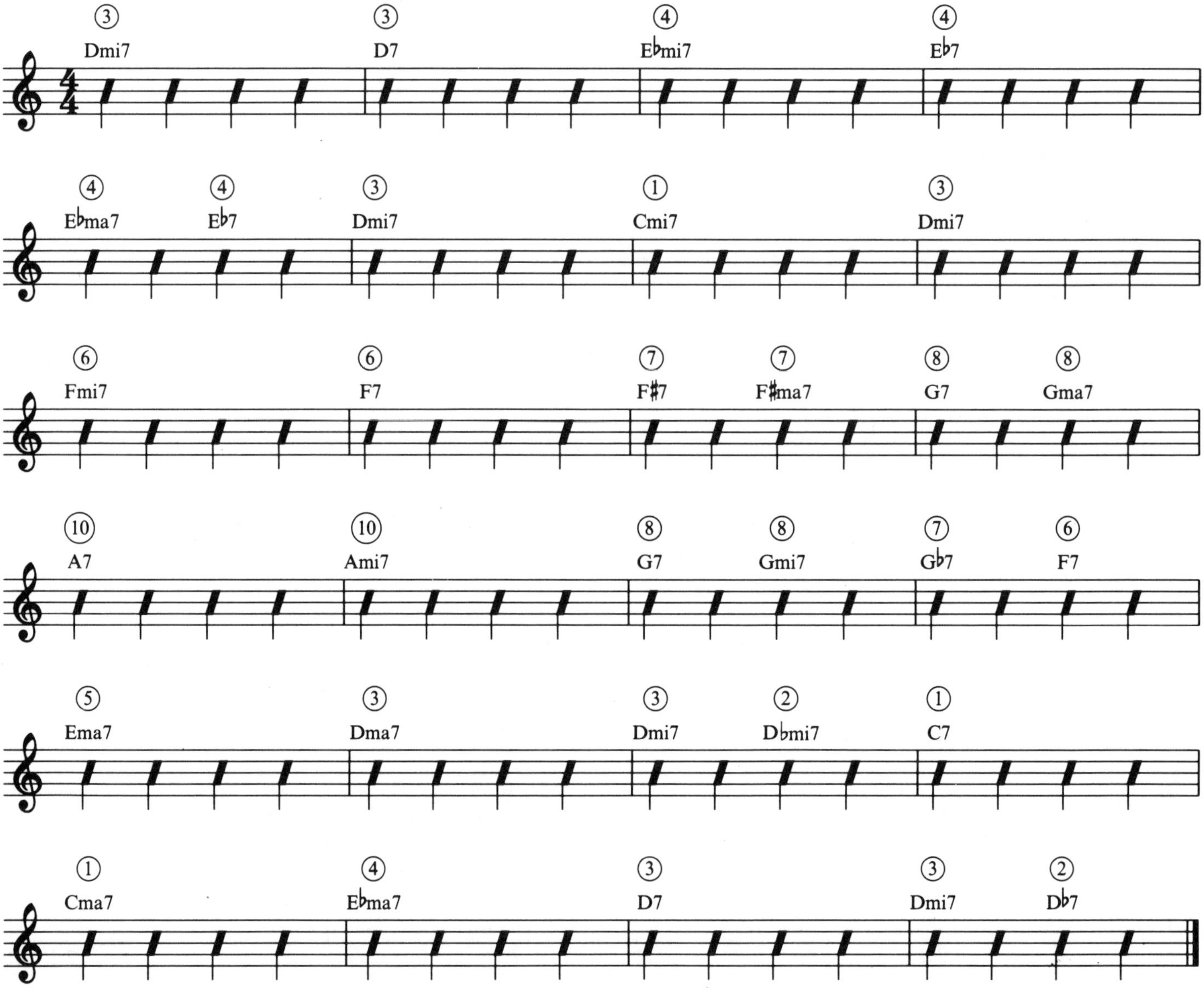

RHYTHM STUDY
Combining the C7 and G7 form with major, minor and dominant sevenths.

Ex. 12

Ex. 13

CHORDS WITH ALTERATIONS
The altered fifth.

The fifth of a chord may be either raised or lowered a half step (one fret). The reasons for doing this may be: 1. to create more tension before resolution, 2. to add more dissonance to the music, 3. to create a smoother resolution.

The C7 chord is constructed:

If the C7 would resolve to an F MA7 chord, the G would move a whole step (2 frets) to the F:

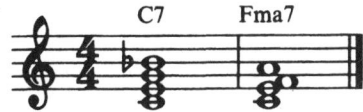 

If the fifth in the C7 chord is lowered, the Gb would move a half step (one fret) to the F:

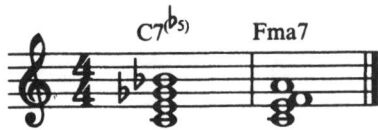 

In order to play most chords on the guitar, the order of the notes must be changed to make them playable. The voicing for the C7 on the preceding page is written in the root position, with the root on the bottom and the notes stacked above it from lowest to highest. This voicing is very clear to look at, and can be played on the piano but not on the guitar.

ROOT POSITION
piano voicing:  changed to be playable on guitar:

Notice that in this voicing the fifth is the lowest note in the chord. This the C7 voicing the book has been using so far:

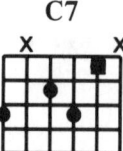

To make a C7(b5) (C seventh with a lowered fifth), the G is moved down one fret keeping the other notes where they were:

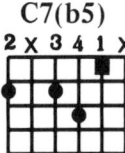

To make a C7(#5) (C seventh with a raised fifth), the G is moved up one fret from G to G#:

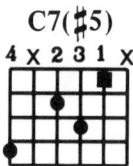

PRACTICE EXERCISES

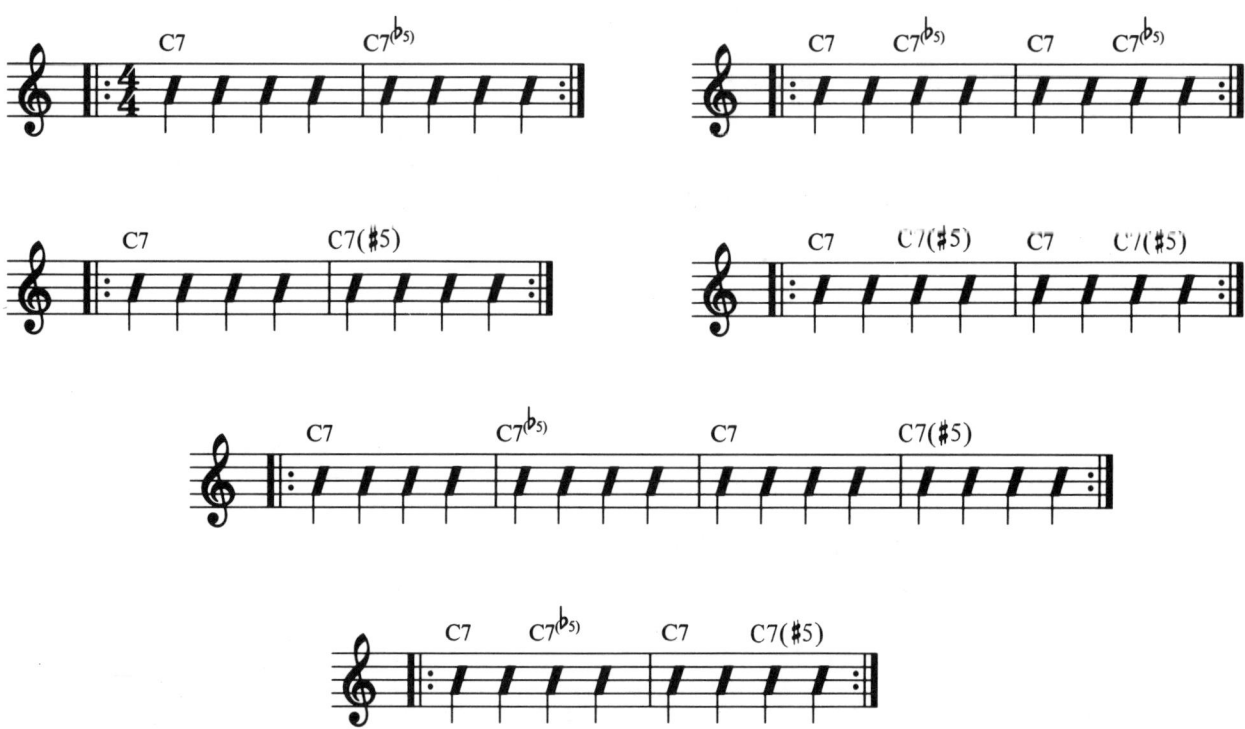

THE G7 FORM
With raised or lowered fifth.

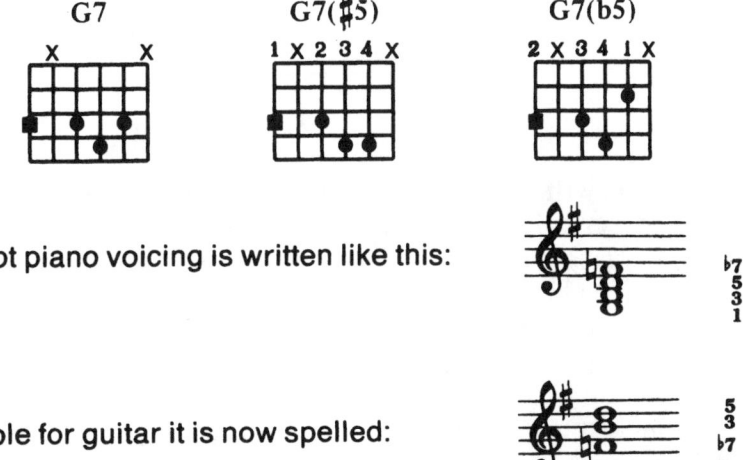

The G7 in the root piano voicing is written like this:

To make it playable for guitar it is now spelled:

PRACTICE EXERCISES

There are some rhythmic figures that can cause trouble for the guitarist. One of these is the figure that has the chord change on the last half beat of the measure:

The way this music is written, you are expected to play a G7 on the first half of the fourth beat and a G7♯5 on the second half. The chord on the upbeat is probably very important and is accented. However, it you try to play this as written: 1) you might be late for the G7♯5, 2) you might hit some chord other than the G7♯5, especially if it is a fast tempo and 3) the G7 on the first half of the beat might lessen the impact of the accented chord.

Many guitarists solve this problem by playing the above figure as follows:

This results in a cleaner approach to the altered chord, and will help playability at a fast tempo.

If you have enough technique and are sure you can pull it off at the tempo played, it can be fun to play the first example as written. If you do remember to accent the chord change on the upbeat.

Ex. 14

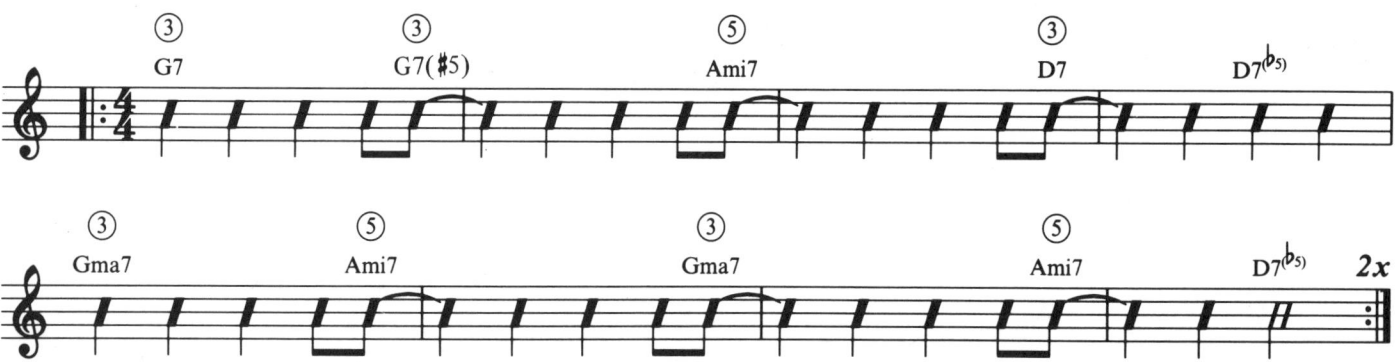

REVIEW

This exercise includes all chords and rhythms studied so far.

Ex. 15

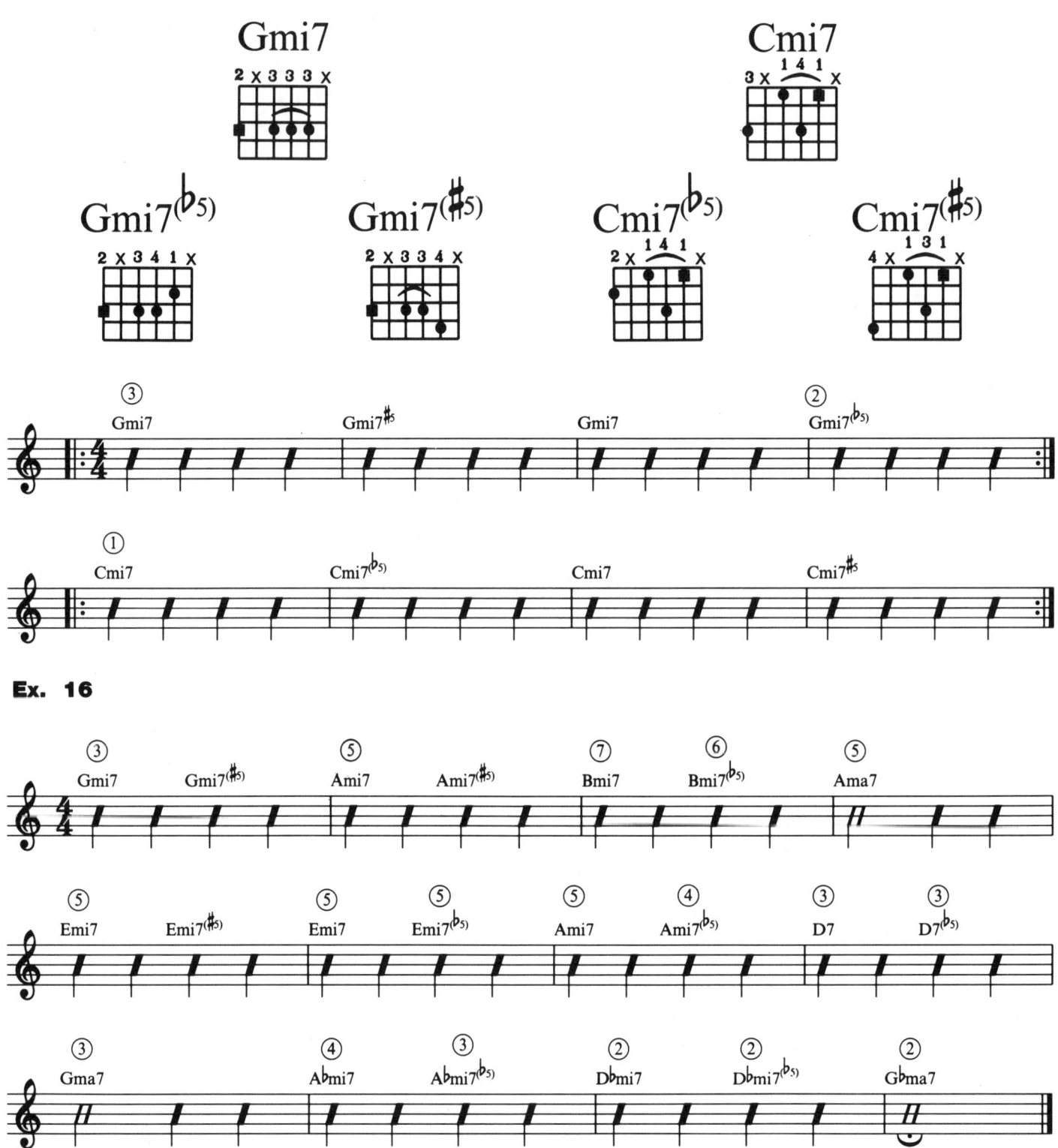

THE MAJOR 7th CHORD
WITH RAISED AND LOWERED FIFTHS

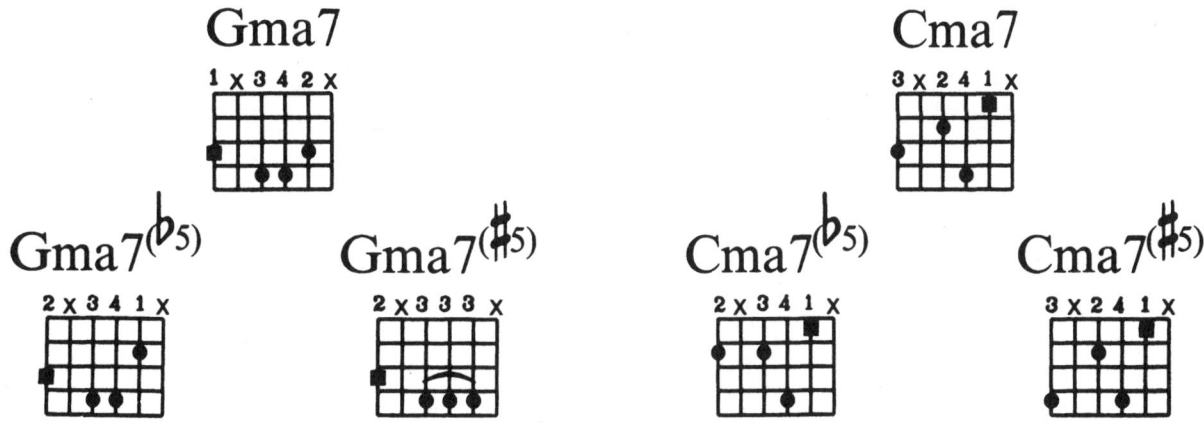

Major sevenths with altered fifths are not used often in older music. This is a relatively modern chord used in jazz and jazz-fusion music. It can create a moody, spacey effect.

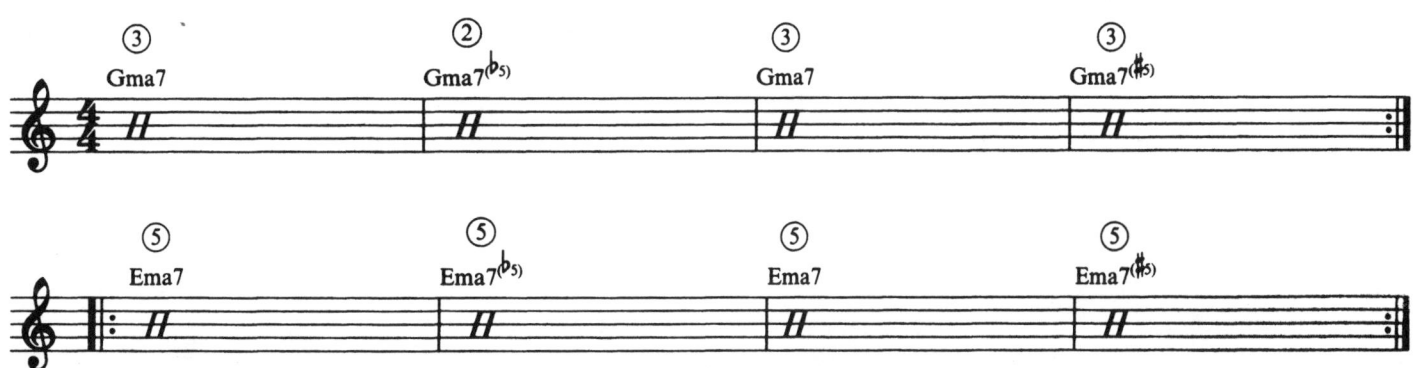

NOTE: The major sevenths with altered fifths based on the C7 form are hard to play below the fifth fret unless you have a large hand.

 Ex. 17

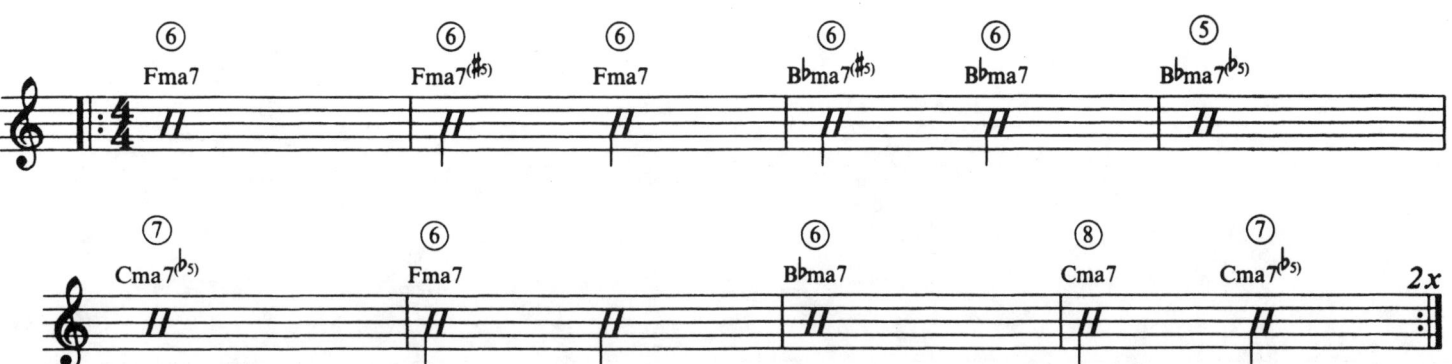

31

REVIEW
CHORDS WITH ALTERED FIFTHS

Ex. 18

Ex. 19

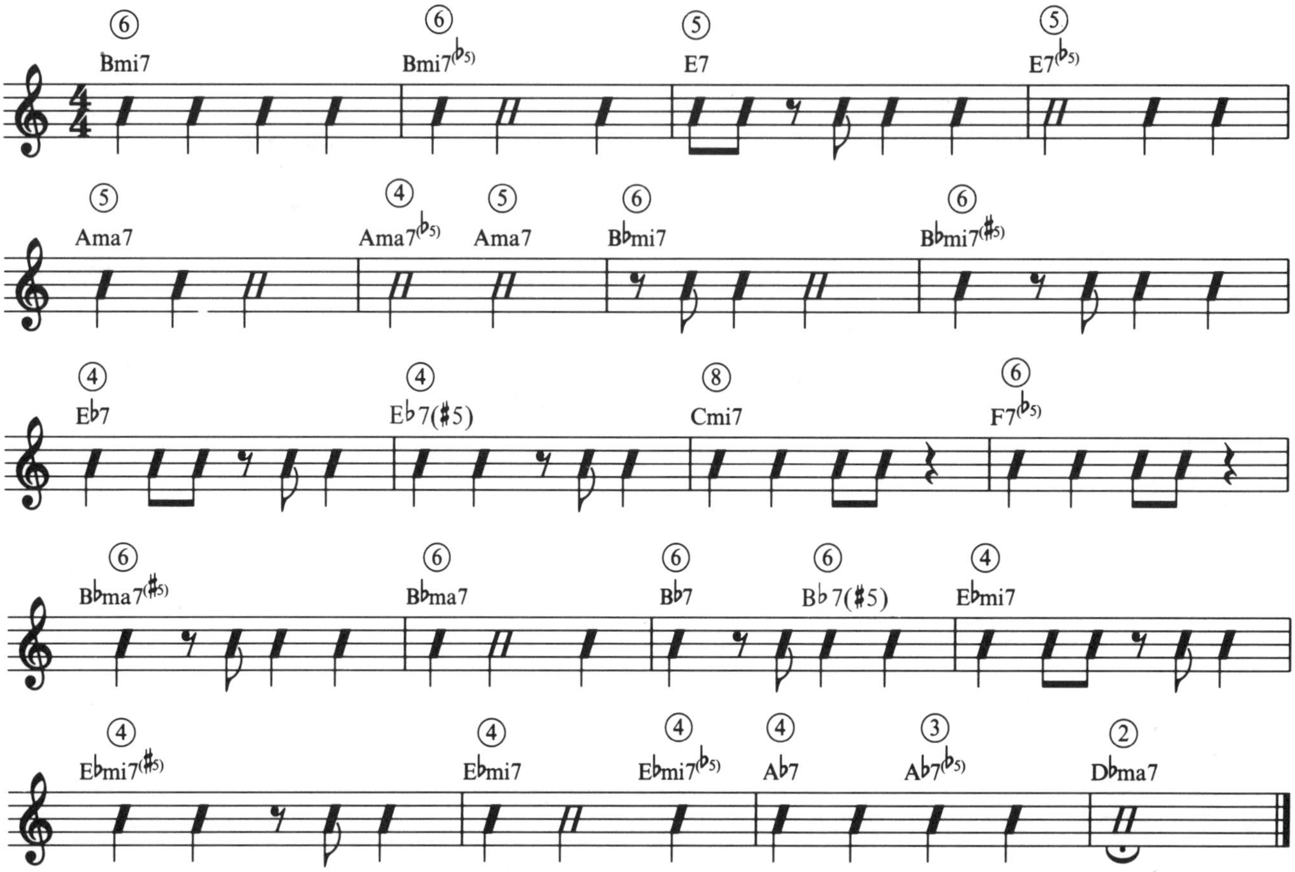

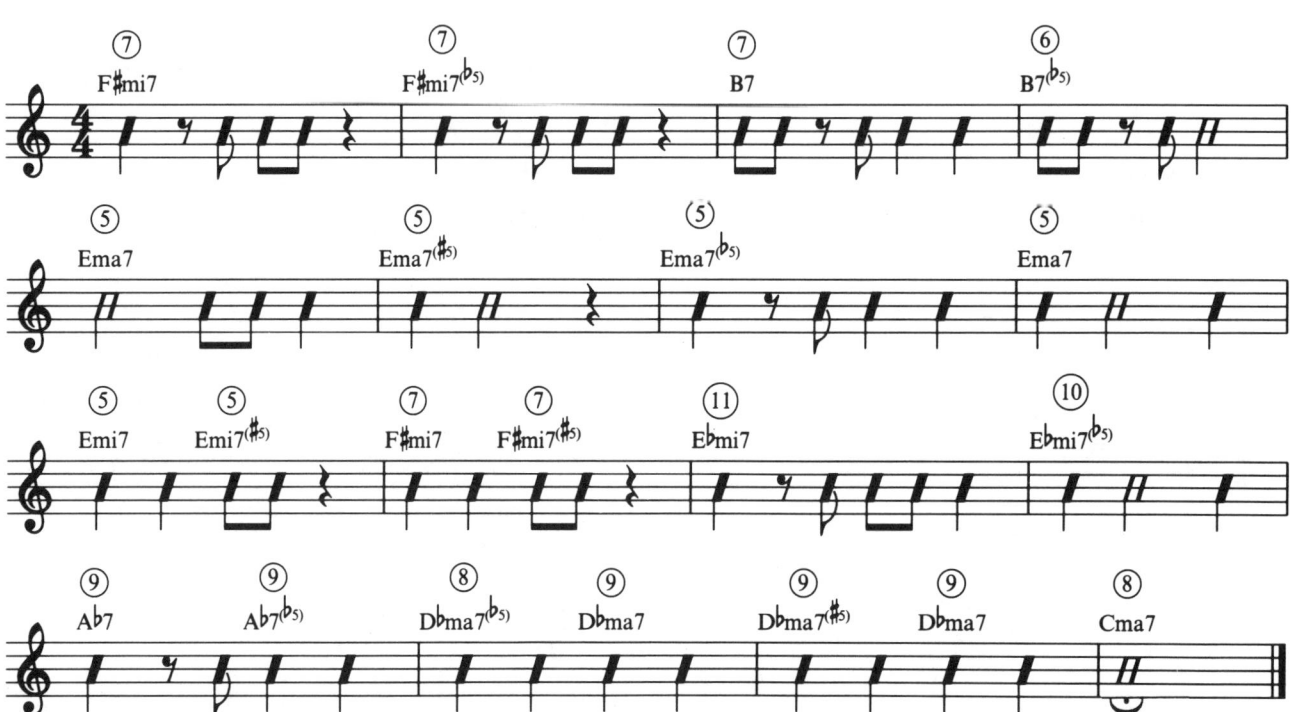

SYNCOPATED LATIN RHYTHMS

When accents happen in-between the beats as well as on the beats, it is called syncopation. These syncopations can be tied through the following beat or into the next measure. Be sure to refer to the taped versions of these examples to hear the correct rhythms.

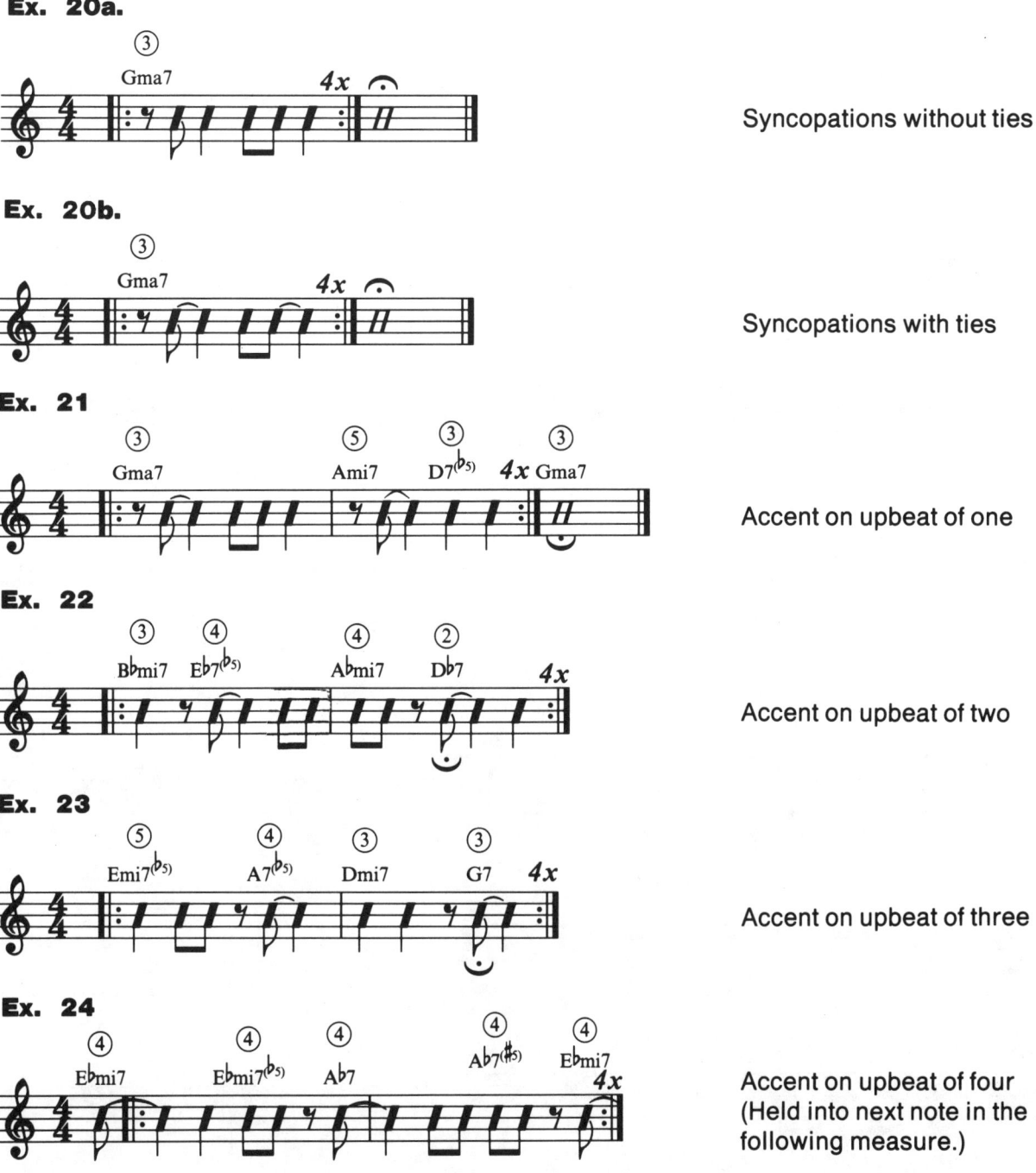

Ex. 20a. — Syncopations without ties

Ex. 20b. — Syncopations with ties

Ex. 21 — Accent on upbeat of one

Ex. 22 — Accent on upbeat of two

Ex. 23 — Accent on upbeat of three

Ex. 24 — Accent on upbeat of four (Held into next note in the following measure.)

Two of the most common Latin rhythms used today are the "Bossa Nova" (may be shortened to "Bossa") and the "Samba." The Bossa rhythms sound best on the guitar with all down strokes, or picking each note individually at the same time for a piano-like attack. There are two ways of writing syncopated Bossa rhythms. Both will be used so that you will be familiar with them when they appear in ensemble charts:

The Samba is faster than a Bossa and uses up and down strokes and muted strings. The pressure of the left hand on the strings is released, but the fingers remain touching the strings. When the strings are strummed at this time, a drum-like effect is created. The right hand strums up and down continually on even eighth notes:

Strum:

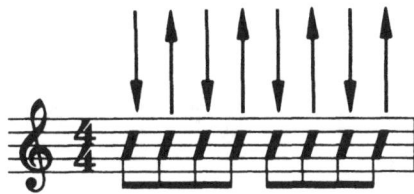

The left hand keeps the formation of the chord being played when releasing the string pressure.

NOTE: ≢ = Push down strings

⨯ = Release pressure (mute)

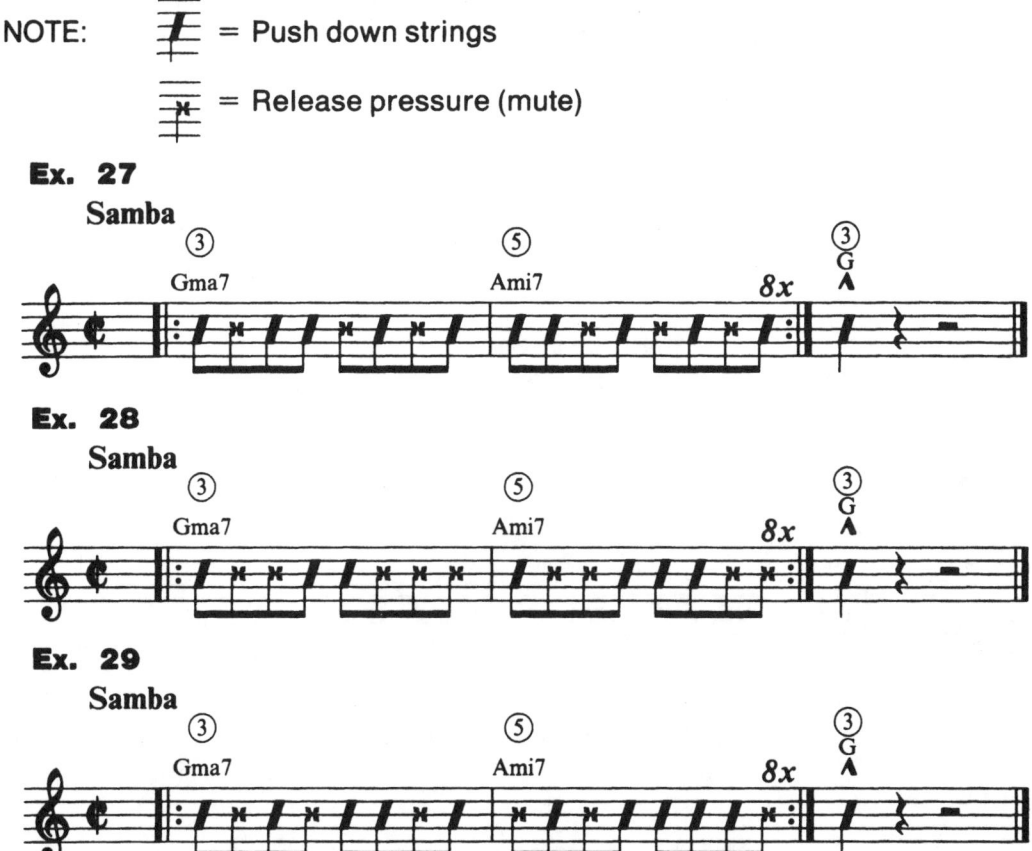

Some Sambas go very fast. For this type of music, the rhythm may be simplified.

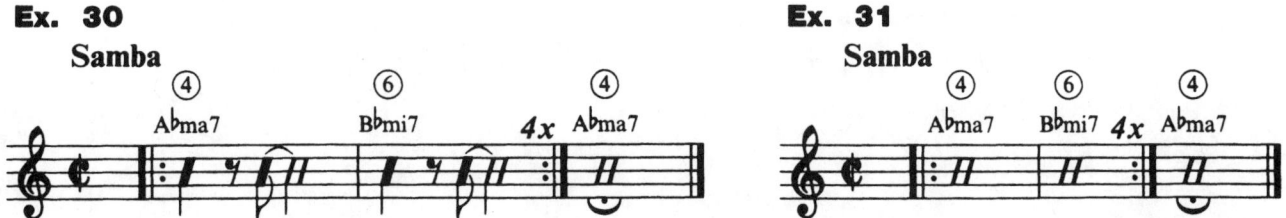

One problem with reading some Latin charts for ensemble is that some arrangers don't write the exact rhythms. Therefore, you must improvise the rhythm and find something that works with the rest of the music.

Here are two examples of Samba chart styles. If these would be played as written it would be the incorrect style:

In reading guitar charts, the player must decide when it is best to play what is written, and when to improvise.

Some arrangers take the approach of writing a Samba similar to Example 28 except the muted markings are left out and replaced by eighth rests:

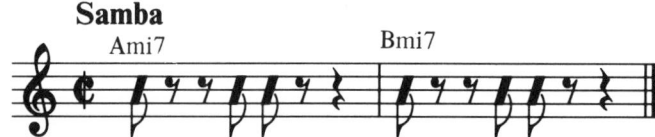

You can play the previous example like Example 28 if you wish. But if you want a cleaner sound, just play it as written, with the rests. Then you would strum it as follows:

Ex. 32

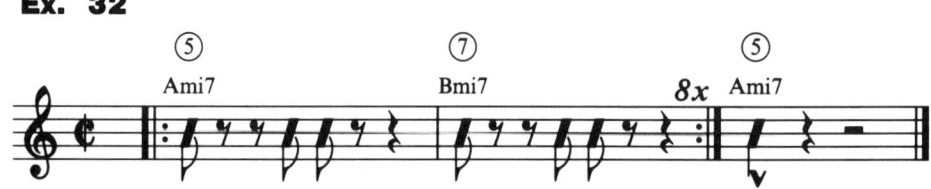

Here's another variation of this Samba rhythm:

Ex. 33

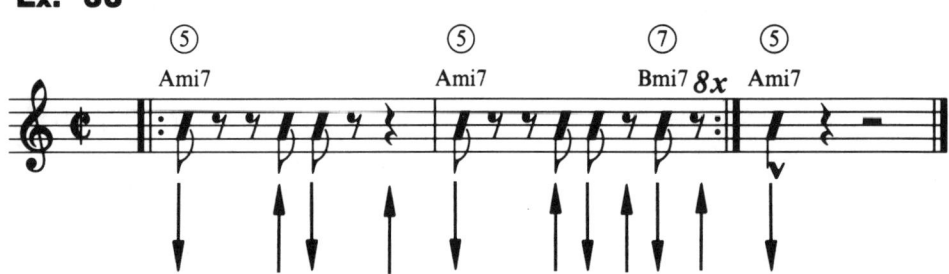

Since much of what the guitarist does in a Latin context changes continually throughout the song, memorize each of the previous Samba rhythms. Play through Example 34, using each of the rhythms exclusively. When you're ready, turn the guitar channel off and play with the bass and drummer, changing the rhythms at random.

Ex. 34

THE NINTH CHORD

The ninth chord is constructed by adding the ninth degree of the scale to the seventh chord. If the ninth is added to a major seventh chord, the new chord becomes a major ninth chord. Added to the minor seventh, a minor ninth chord is created. The dominant seventh becomes a dominant ninth. See page 11 for a review of the theory behind this chord construction.

Many times on guitar, it is impossible to play a complete ninth, eleventh or thirteenth chord. One or more notes of the chord must be deleted. The fifth is the least important note (if it's unaltered) so one common voicing for the 9th has the fifth left out:

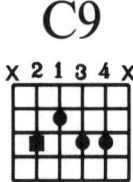   

The ninth note may be raised or lowered just like the fifth:

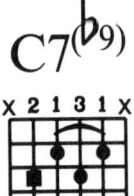   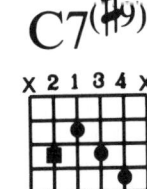

Another way of playing the ninth chord includes the fifth. Notice the octave in which it must be played:

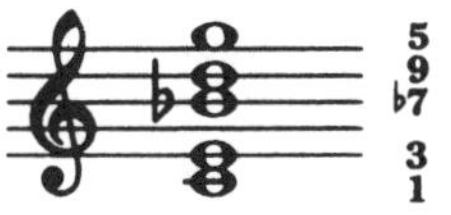

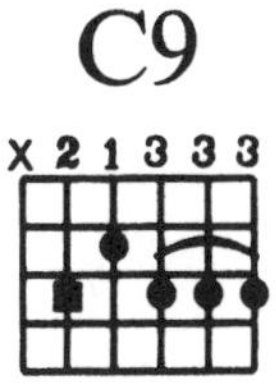

This ninth voicing works well for heavy strumming because there isn't a muted string on top. If you go back and forth to chords with an altered ninth, the ninth chord with no fifth from preceding page works better.

Ex. 35
Bossa

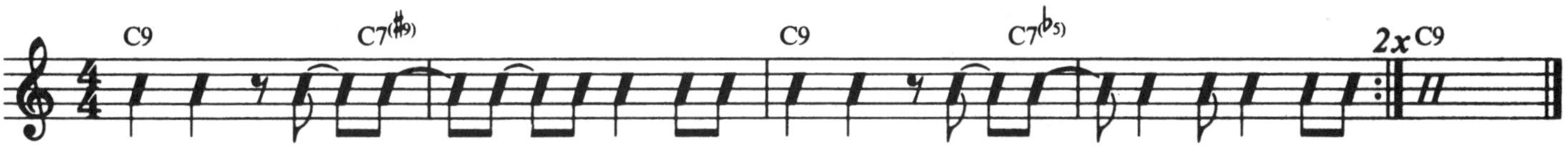

Ex. 36
Bossa

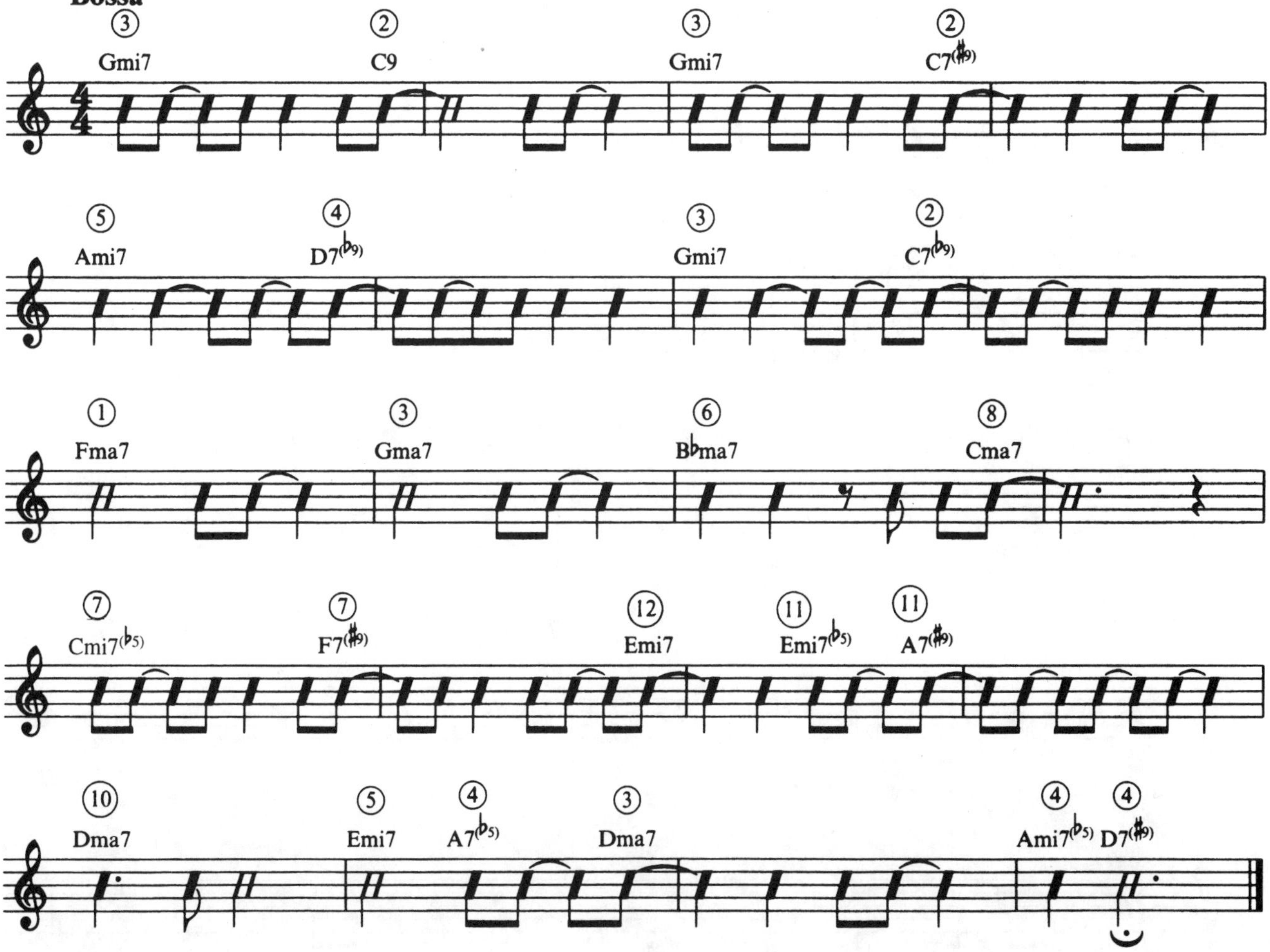

THE NINTH BASED ON THE G7 FORM

This is a great sounding chord which is used regularly by most blues players. It's easy to go to the C9 voicing which is right across from it. There is no need to jump way up the neck to play a G9 from the C9 when using the same ninth voicing to play in different keys. The minor and major ninths based on this chord will not be discussed since they do not sound like ninth chords and can be confused with other forms.

Bar the fourth finger without flattening the other fingers.

If this is too hard for you, then try the two voicings without the root on the high E string:

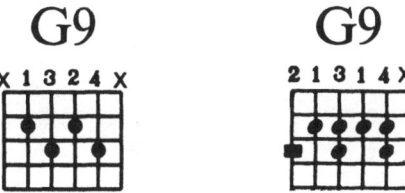

When there is a chord like the one on the left without a root, you must visualize and remember where the root is so you can move the chord around the neck. In most music the ninth chord may be played as a substitute for the dominant seventh chord.

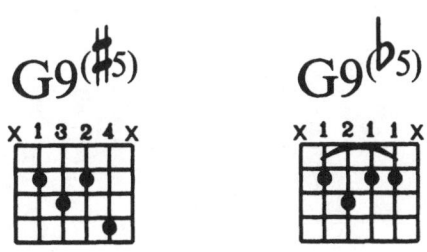

This blues exercise is in 12/8. In this style there are 12 eighth notes per measure. Or, you count it as four quarter note beats per measure with a triplet on each beat. A measure in 12/8 looks like this:

Sometimes you'll see it like this:

Which means you read in 4/4 but play like the first example in 12/8.

Ex. 39
Bluesy

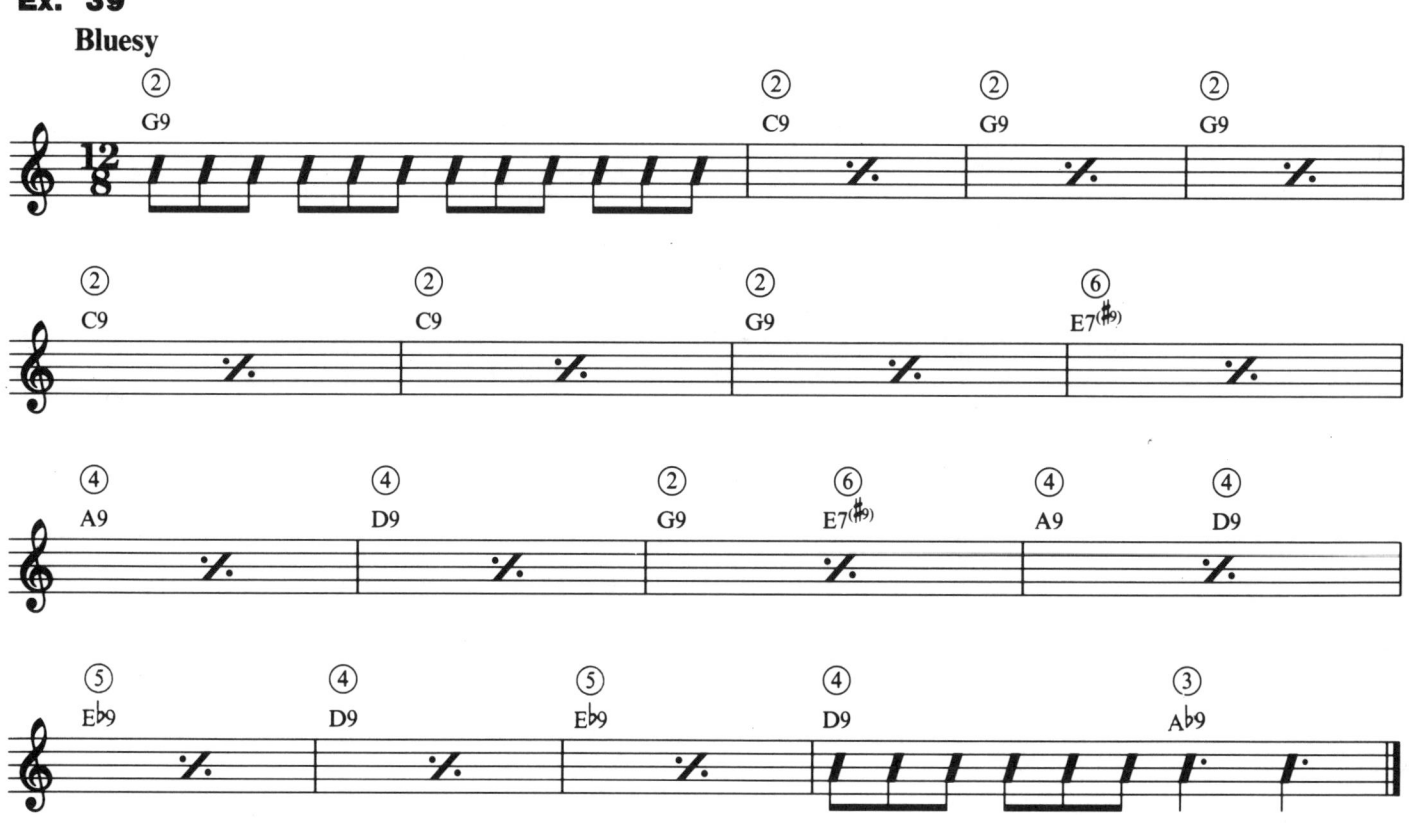

NOTE: ·/. means play the same rhythm as the previous measure but with the chord that is above the new measure.

There are some variations on the 12/8 strum that can make the music more interesting. These examples are in 6/8. Listen to the taped examples before playing them. The second of the six beats is divided into two parts.

Ex. 40

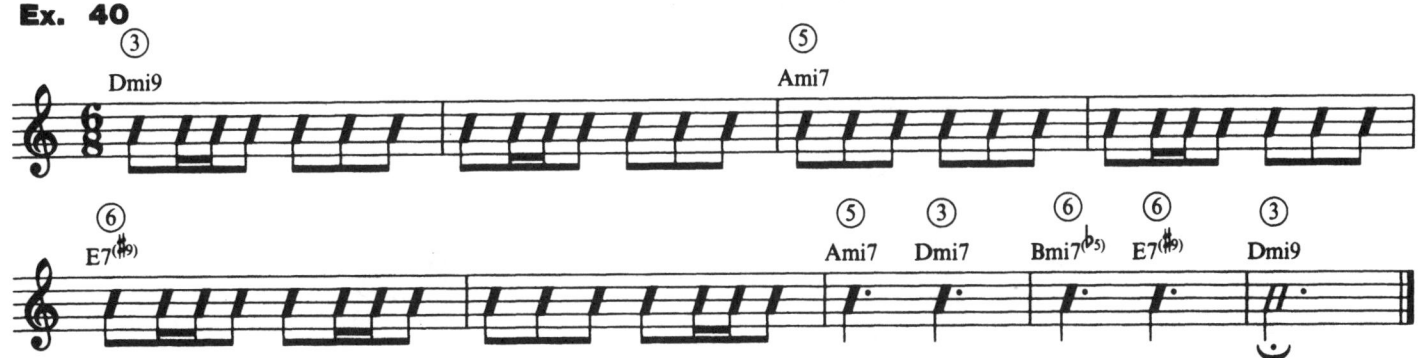

The first chord of every set of 3 can be accented. Usually the accent on the first and third beats is a long one and the accent on the second and fourth beats is a short one. This creates the "back beat" feel. "Simile" means carry on the same rhythmic idea with the new chords.

Ex. 41

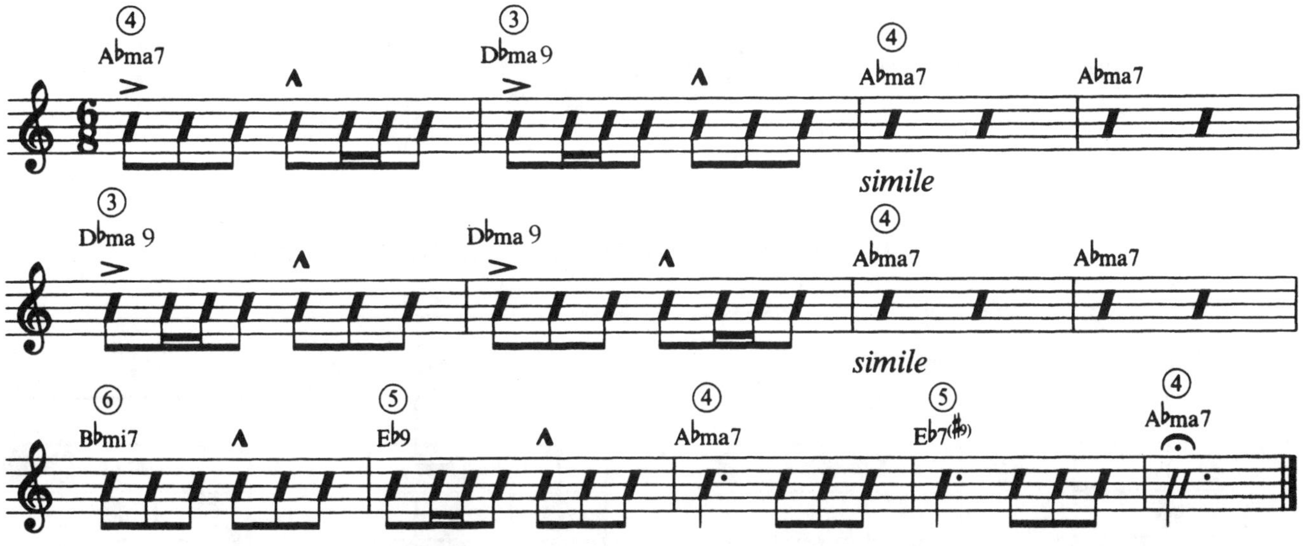

Ex. 42 Interesting patterns can be made by replacing some chords with rests.

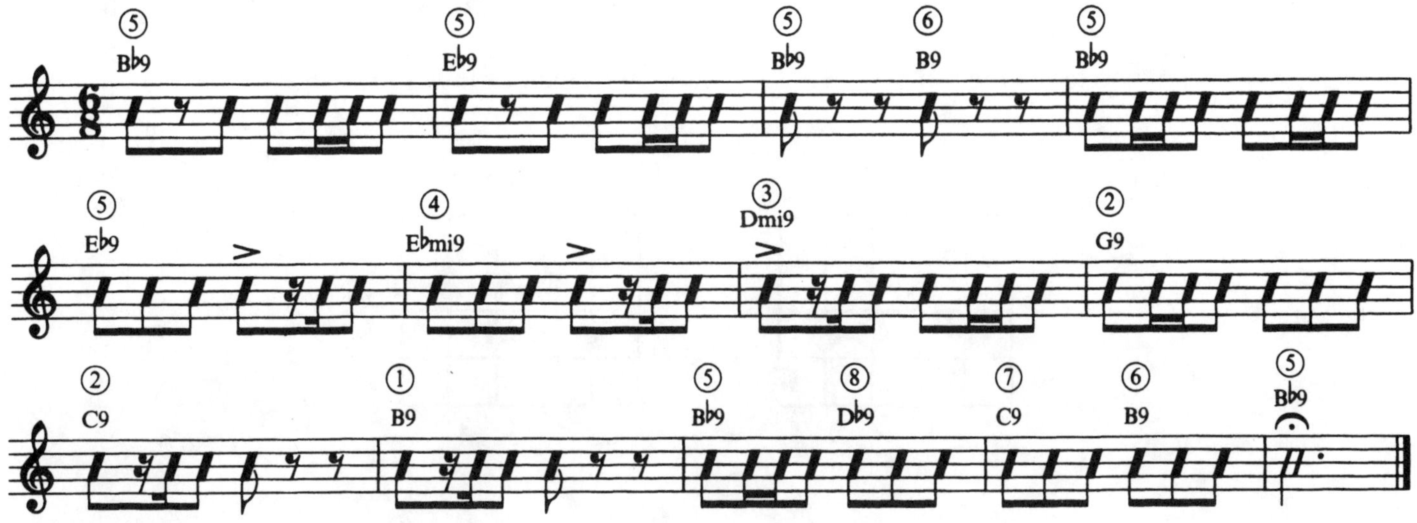

CHORDS WITH MULTIPLE ALTERATIONS

When reading a chart and a chord comes along with more than one alteration, it can catch the guitarist off guard. Here is an easy system to manipulate the combinations of raised and lowered fifths and ninths.

Find the fifth and ninth in this C9 form.

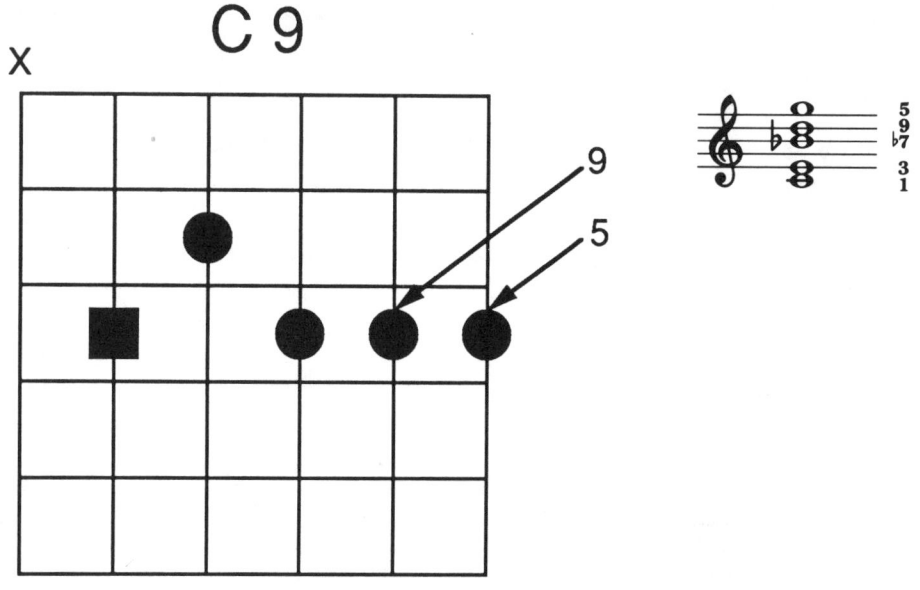

Memorize where the 5 and 9 are. By raising and lowering these two notes the following chords can be created.

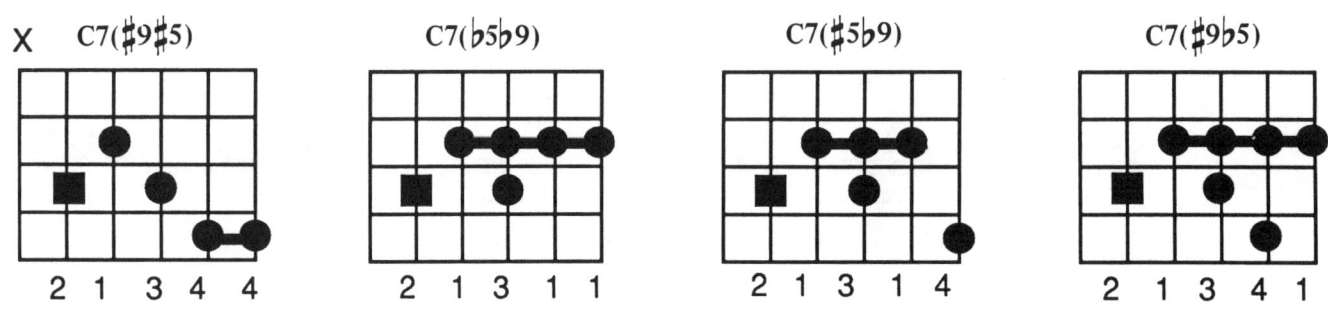

You can also leave the ninth in its natural state and raise or lower the 5th.

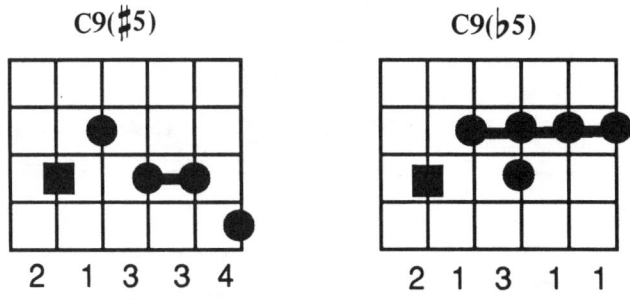

44

DOUBLE ALTERATION PRACTICE

REMEMBER...

1. ...where the root of the chord is located.

2. ...the ninth is located on the second (B) string.

3. ...the fifth is located on the first (E) string.

4. ..."up" is toward the pickups. "Down" is toward the tuning gears.

This piece starts out as a "jazz piece" and changes to a "bossa" half way through.

Ex. 43

Making double alterations on the G7 form is a little more complex, since the 5 and 9 don't line up on the same fret as on the C7 form.

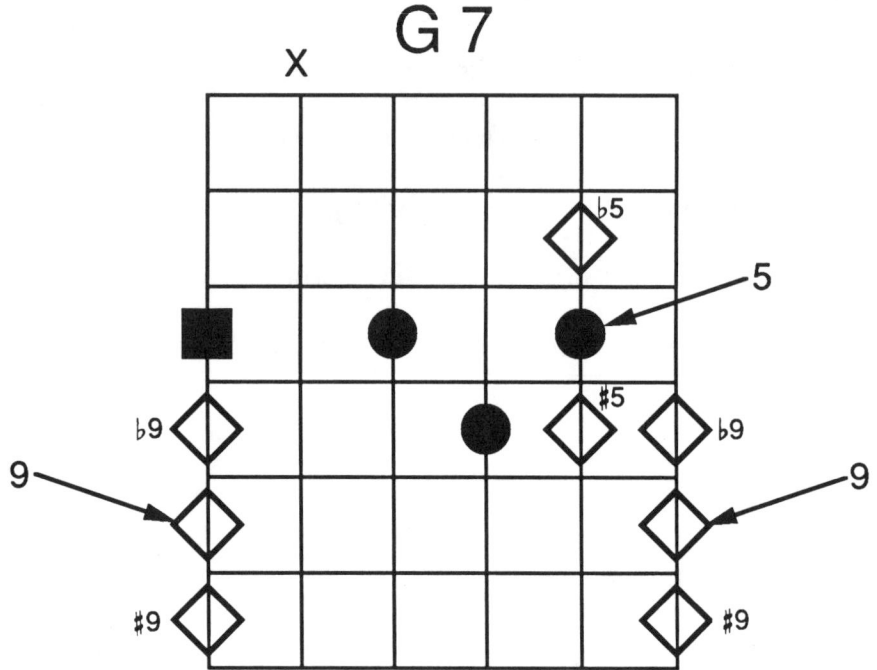

The easiest double-altered chords based on this form are the G7(♭9♯5) and G7(♯9♯5).

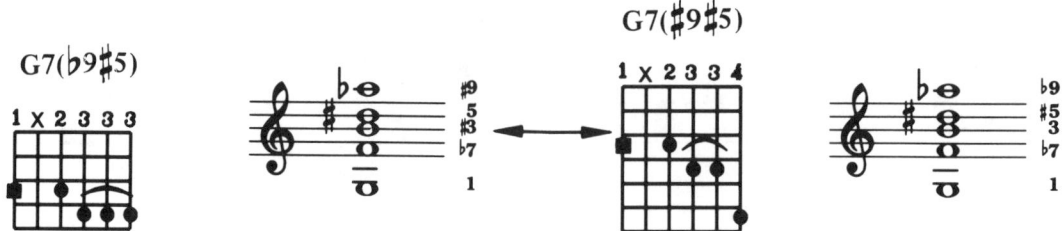

The chords based on this form with the lowered fifth and altered ninth are either too difficult to play or don't sound good. If you must use this form because of the key, one double-altered chord can usually be substituted for a different double-altered chord. For example, you can substitute a ♯5 for a ♭5 because there is a whole step between these two pitches. This will sound much better than the half-step dissonance created by the (♮) 5.

Ex. 44
Bossa

ELEVENTH AND SUSPENDED FOURTH CHORDS

An eleventh chord has six notes if played in its complete form. Again, as with the ninth chord, a note must be deleted to make it playable on the guitar.

The complete minor eleventh is constructed:

If the fifth is removed, we get a chord which sounds very much like the complete eleventh and can perform the same functions:

This minor eleventh chord can be played:

The dominant eleventh also deletes the fifth:

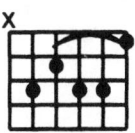 

This is a strange bar with the finger bent and partly on its side. For players that have a hard time with this one, there are some alternatives. The suspended fourth chord can be used as a substitute. This is possible because the fourth is the same pitch as the eleventh (an octave apart). The C9sus4 is the substitute for the C11.

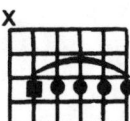 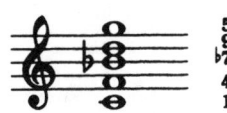

The most basic suspended fourth voicing uses the C7 form by replacing the third (E) with a fourth (F).

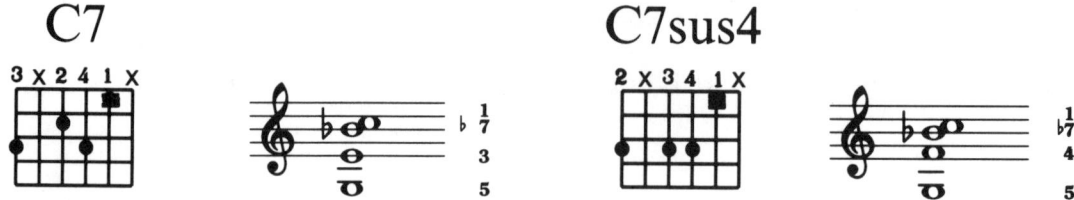

The major eleventh chord sounds strange to to most people and is rarely used. If a form of a major eleventh is played it usually has a raised eleventh:

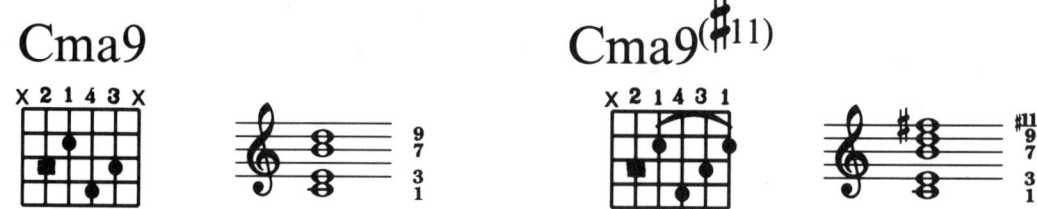

Remember, the #11 means that the 11 was raised from the position it occupies in the major scale: F to F#.

Ex. 47

Jazz Rock

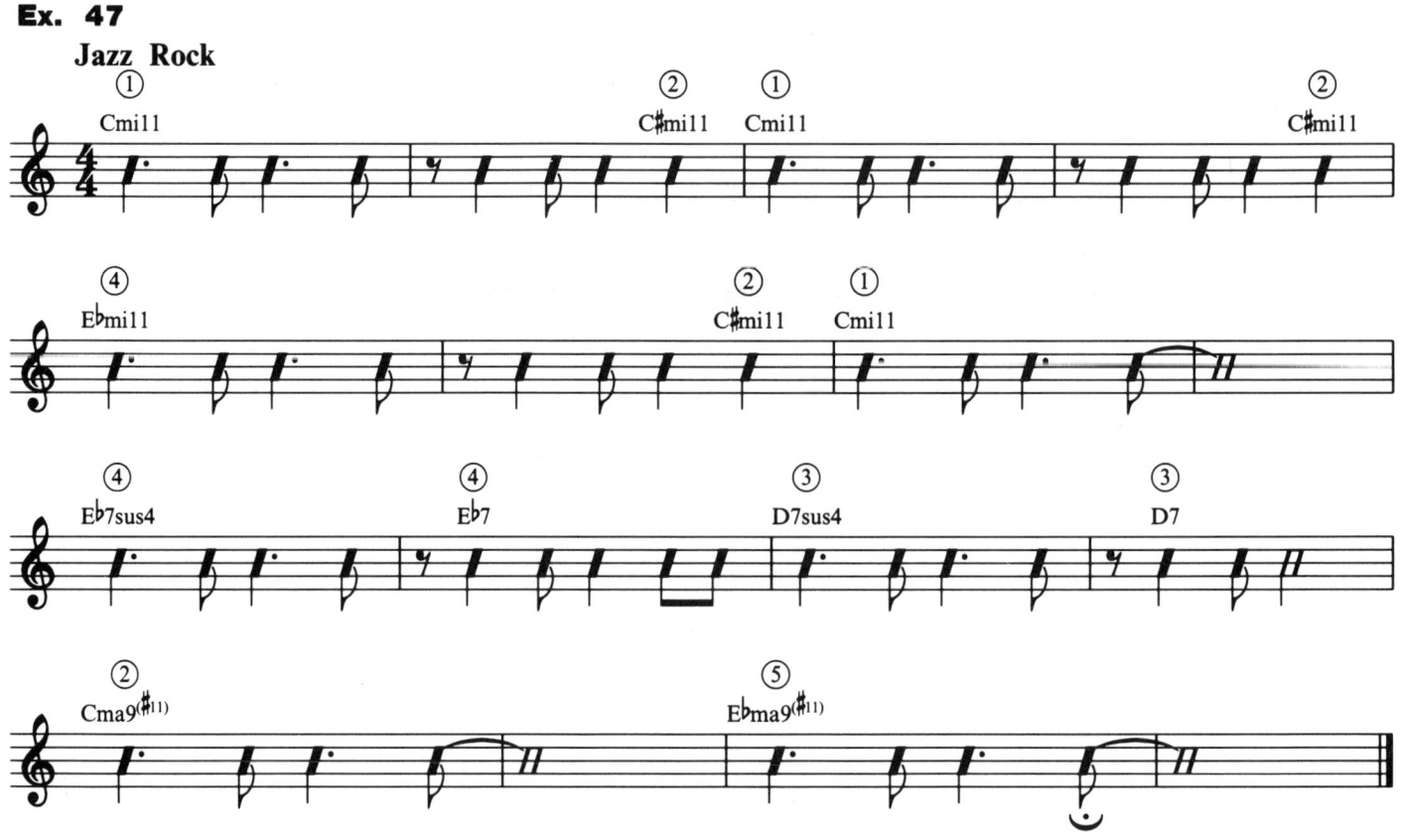

ANOTHER MINOR ELEVENTH: This chord contains both the third and fourth. The third is a minor seventh above the fourth. Normally in an eleventh chord, the eleventh (same pitch as the fourth) is located an octave above the third. Because of the separation of the two important notes, and the presence of the necessary notes, we can call this form an eleventh. It is a great sounding chord and may be a direct substitute for a minor 11th.

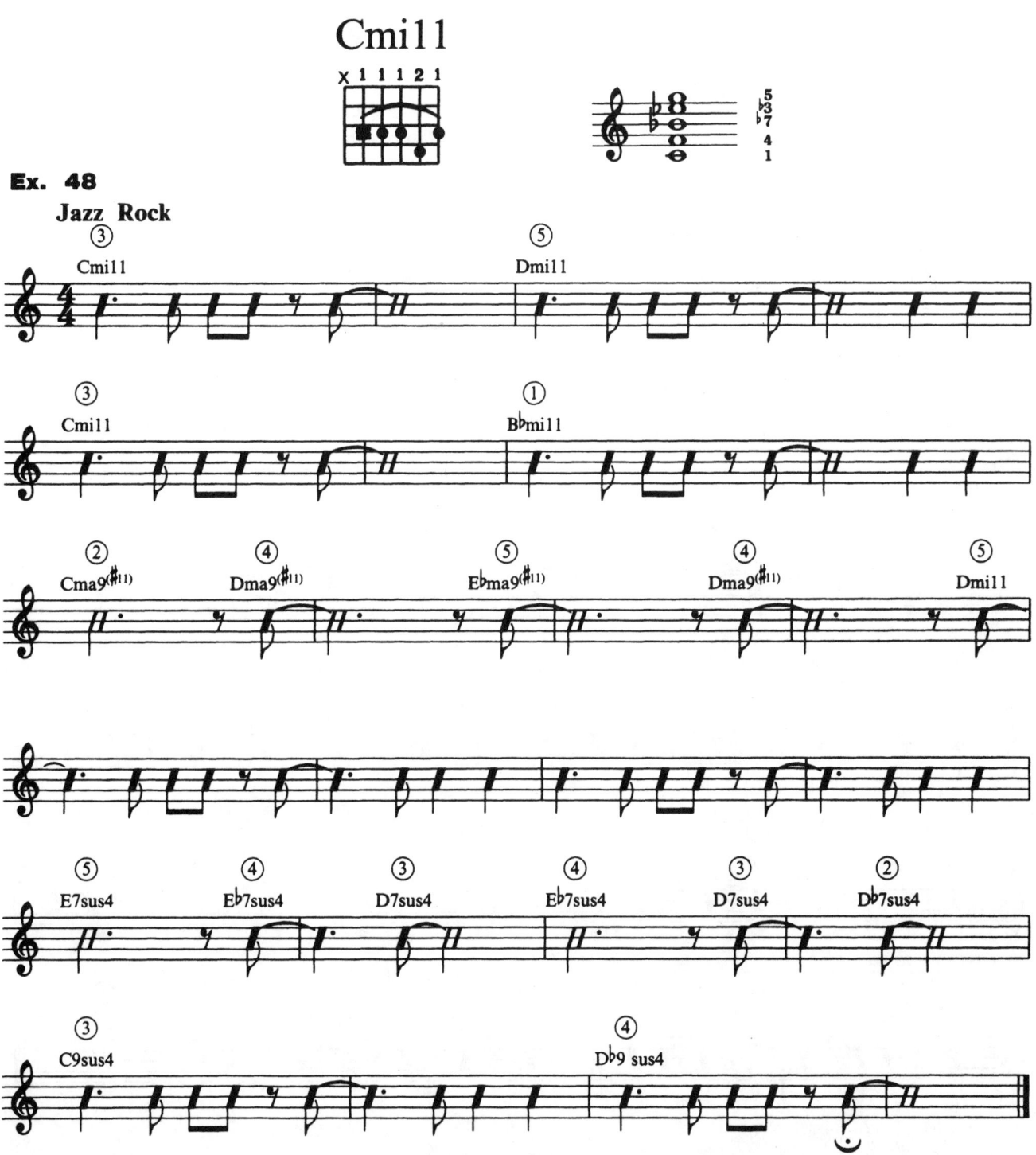

SIXTH CHORDS

The sixth chord is constructed the same way a seventh chord is, but the sixth replaces the seventh.

One of the uses of the sixth chord is to create movement with the seventh chord in situations where the same major or minor chord is played for a long time.

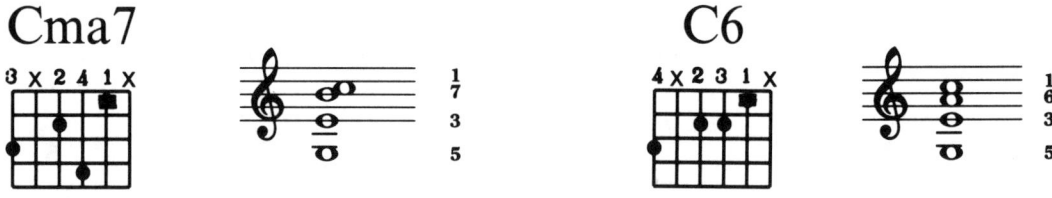

Note: The seventh moves to the sixth.

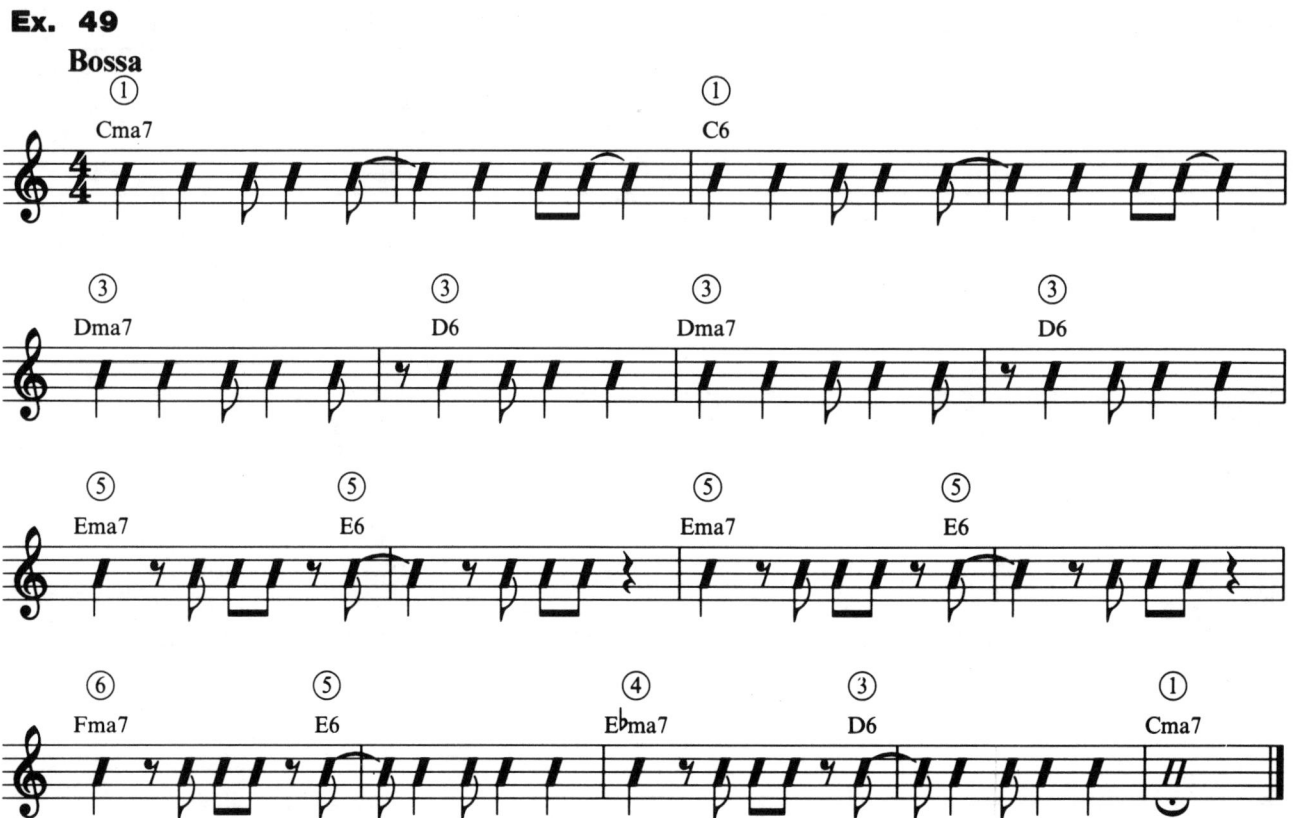

The movement of major seventh to major sixth can also be performed with the G7 form.

Gma7

G6

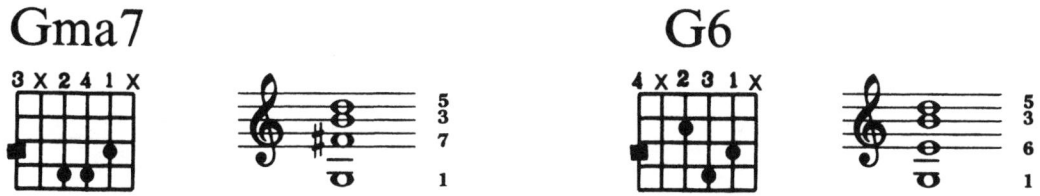

The voicings from page 52 are also included.

Ex. 50

Jazz

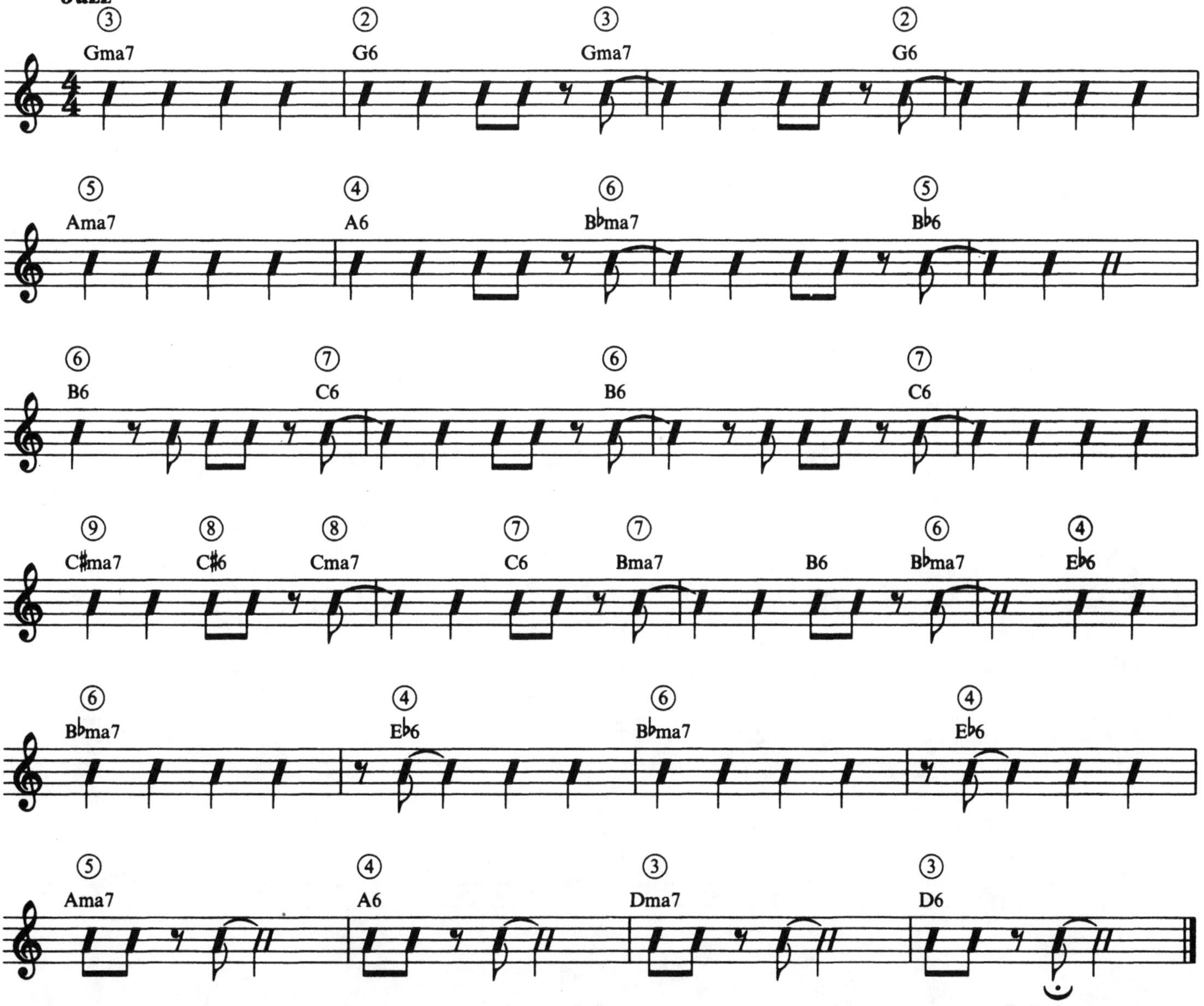

THE SIX/NINE CHORD

This interesting chord consists of a major triad with a sixth and a ninth.

THE MINOR SIXTH

This dark sounding chord is constructed the same as the major sixth, but the lowered third makes it minor.

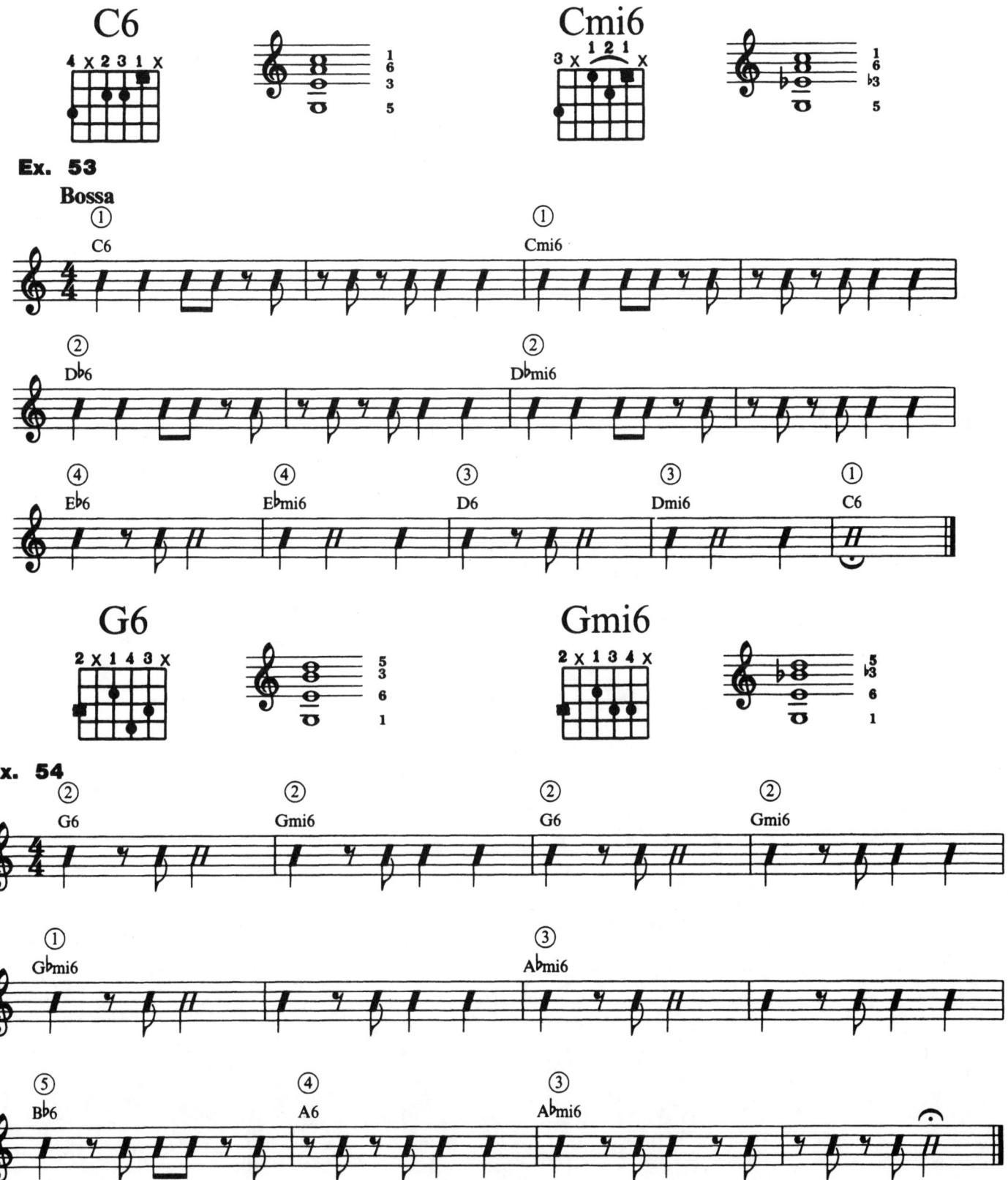

THE MINOR/MAJOR SEVENTH CHORD

This is a strange chord which is not used very often, but when it is, it is an important part of the music. It is constructed from a minor triad with a major seven on top (1, b3, 5, 7). These chords often appear in groups which include the minor seventh and minor six chords. In Example 55, many of the chords change on the upbeat of four. Listen carefully to the tape to get the right feel.

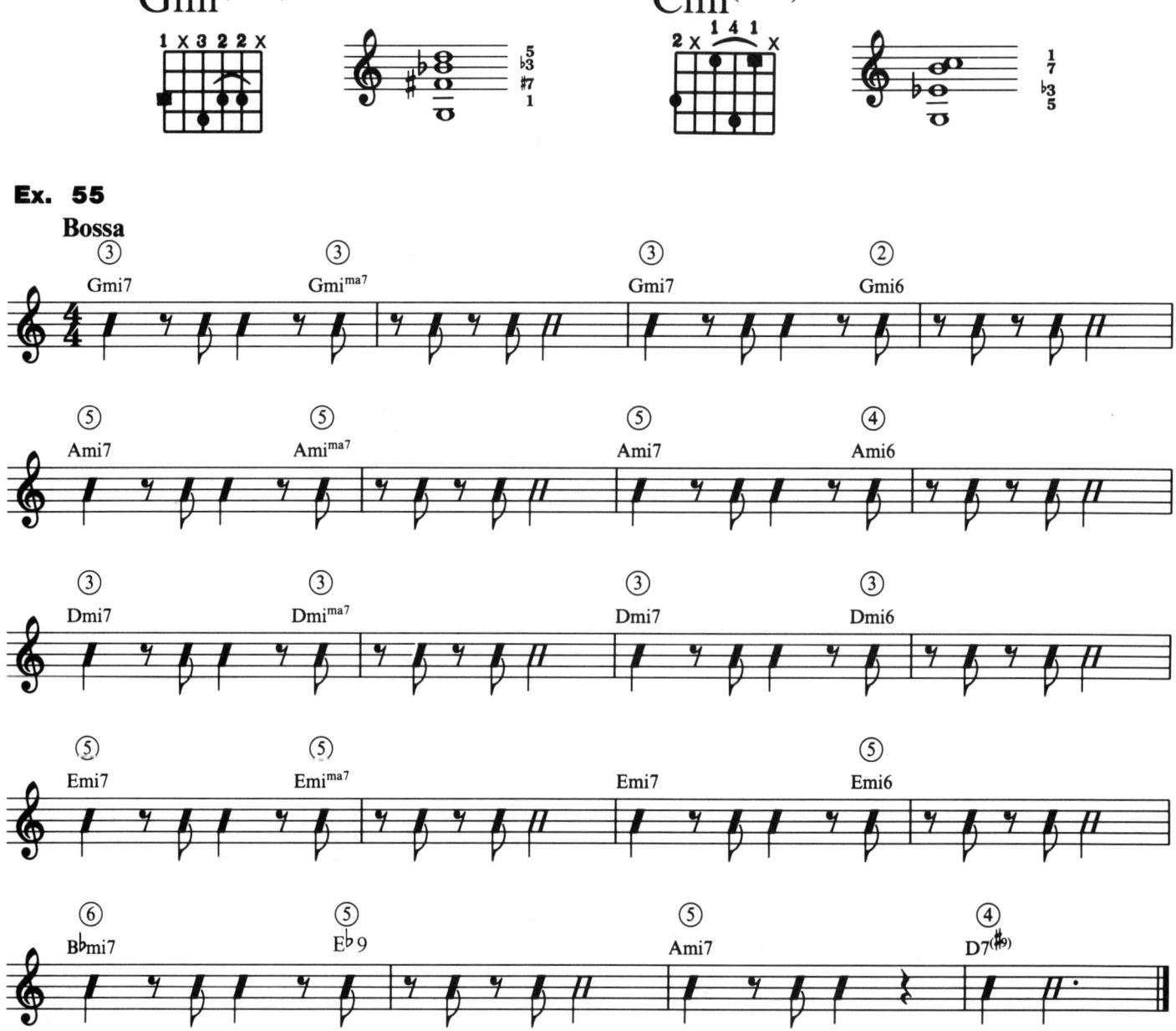

THE THIRTEENTH CHORD

A complete thirteenth chord has 7 notes in it, so the fifth and eleventh are usually left out. The root or the ninth may also be deleted. The third and seventh are never left out because the third is needed to determine the quality of the chord, and the seventh is needed to make the chord dominant. So, the most basic thirteenth chord could be constructed by starting with the third and seventh and adding the thirteenth:

Adding the root.

If you have the technique and like the sound of it, this thirteenth form is more powerful because it also has the ninth in to support the thirteenth. Remember, these chords are based on the G7 form:

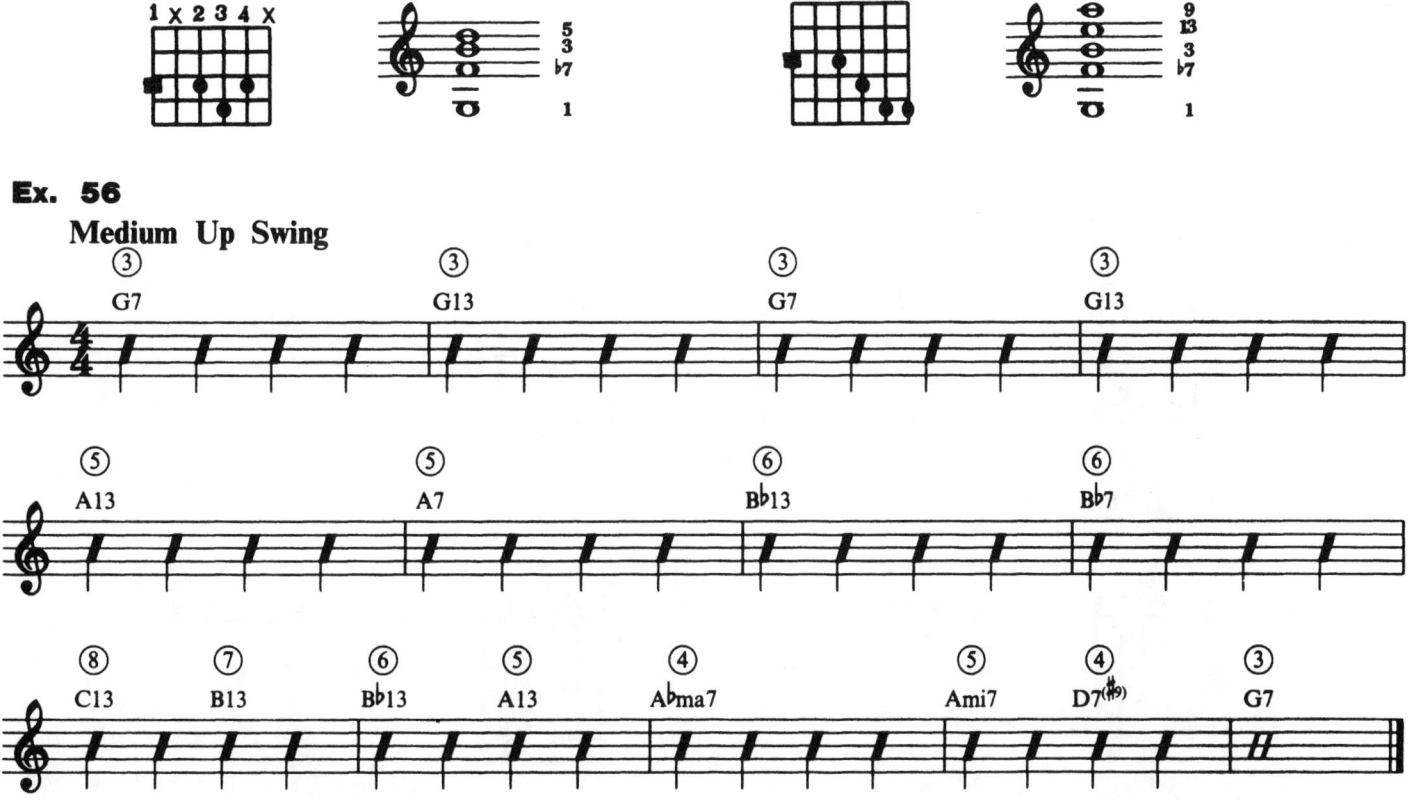

When a chord with a lowered thirteenth is called for, the voicing from page 57 with the thirteenth as the highest note is used.

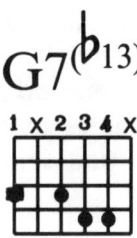

Notice that this form is identical to the form on page 27 for the G7+. This is because D# is the pitch of the raised fifth in a G chord and Eb is the pitch of the lowered thirteenth in a G chord. The octave displacement of some notes and the deletion of others to make music playable on guitar results in some confusing chords with the same form having different names. The thirteenth chord with the ninth from page 57 can be used to make a b7 b13 b9. We learned that +5 is the same pitch as b13, so this chord could also be named 7, +5, b9:

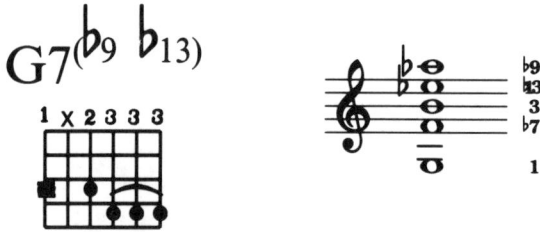

If a thirteenth chord is written with an altered ninth and the thirteenth in its natural state, the root is removed:

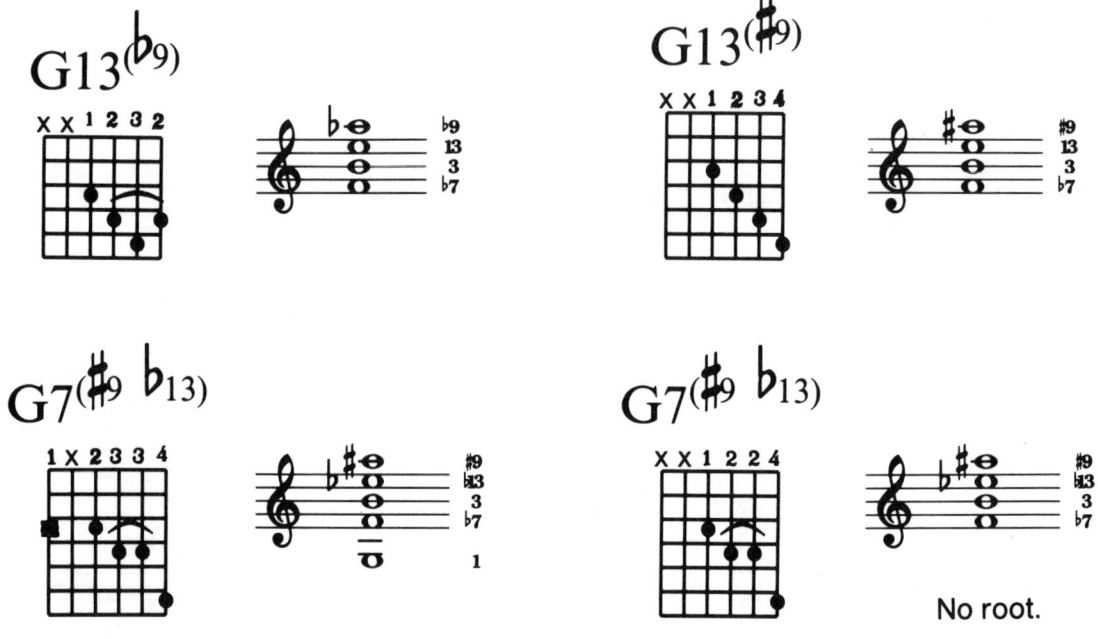

No root.

Altered thirteenths are often preceded by minor chords and followed by major chords making II-V-I (two-five-one) progressions.

Ex. 57

These thirteenth chords are based on the C9 voicing from page 38.

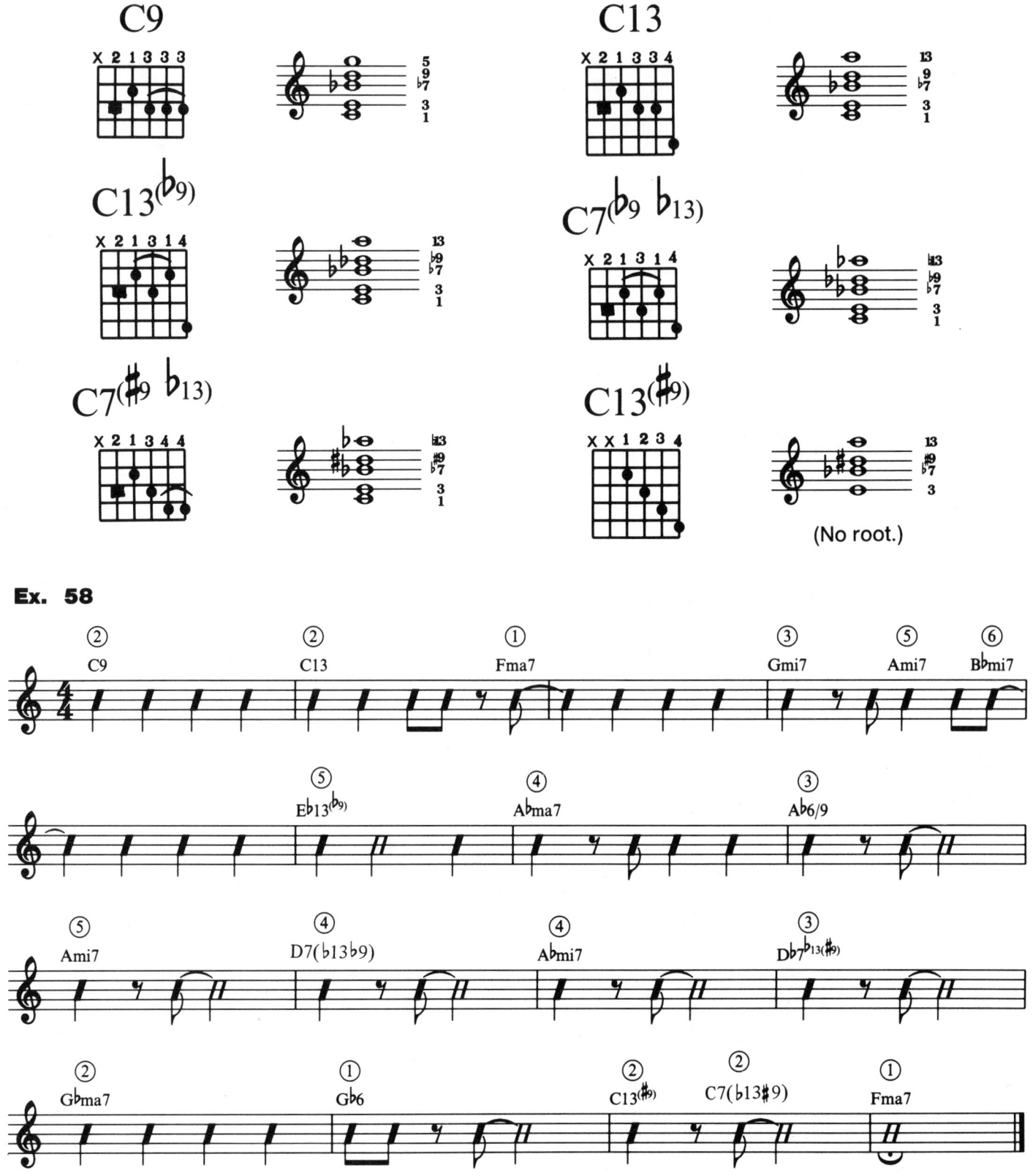

DIMINISHED CHORDS

These chords are constructed using just minor thirds (3 half steps or 3 frets). The distance between each pair of note is the same. The sign for diminished is O.

From C# to E there are 3 frets.
From E to G there are 3 frets, etc.

If we make another inversion of this chord by taking the C# from the bottom and putting it on top, the distance between Bb and C# is a minor third.

Since C# is the same pitch as Db and the chord's root is E, it becomes an E diminished chord.

If we perform this manipulation two more times, we find that the C#o7, Eo7, Go7 and Bbo7 all have the same pitches and are interchangeable. This is important information to have when playing chord charts. The arranger might use an Eo7 voicing for the horns and write Eo7 on the guitar chart. However, it may be very difficult to get to that voicing. If you know that every diminished chord has three other names, it might be easier to play a Go7 than an Eo7. This could eliminate a jump of three frets on the neck.

This diminished seventh chord is based on the G7 voicing. Let's see how to relate diminished chord construction to what we already know.

Start with a Gma7 chord and lower the seventh to get G7.

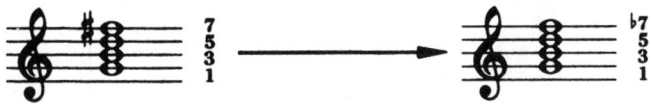

To get Gmi7, lower the third in the G7 chord:

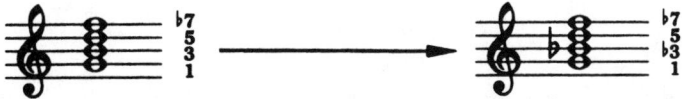

The Gmi7(b5) is built by lowering the fifth in the Gm7 chord. This chord is also known as the half-diminished chord (∅):

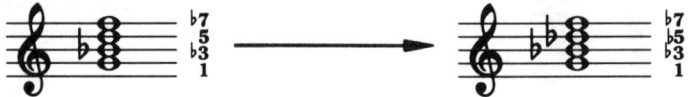

To get a diminished seventh chord, the lowered seventh in Gmi7(b5) is lowered again:

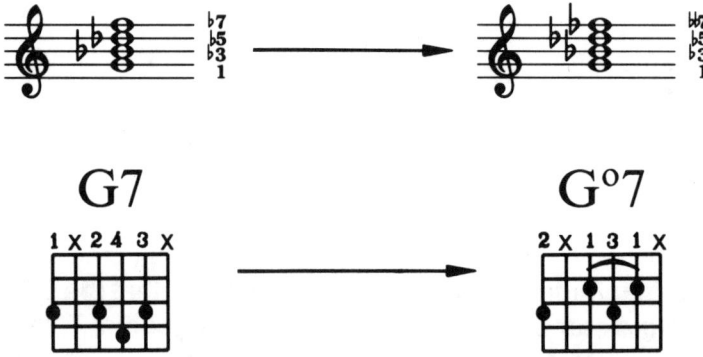

(Could also be labeled Bbo7, Dbo7 or Eo7.)

Now practice (and memorize) all the chords in the cycle from major seventh to diminished seventh. Say the name of each chord as you play it. Look at it on your guitar as you play it so that you coordinate the sound of the chord, the shape of your hand, and the name of the chord.

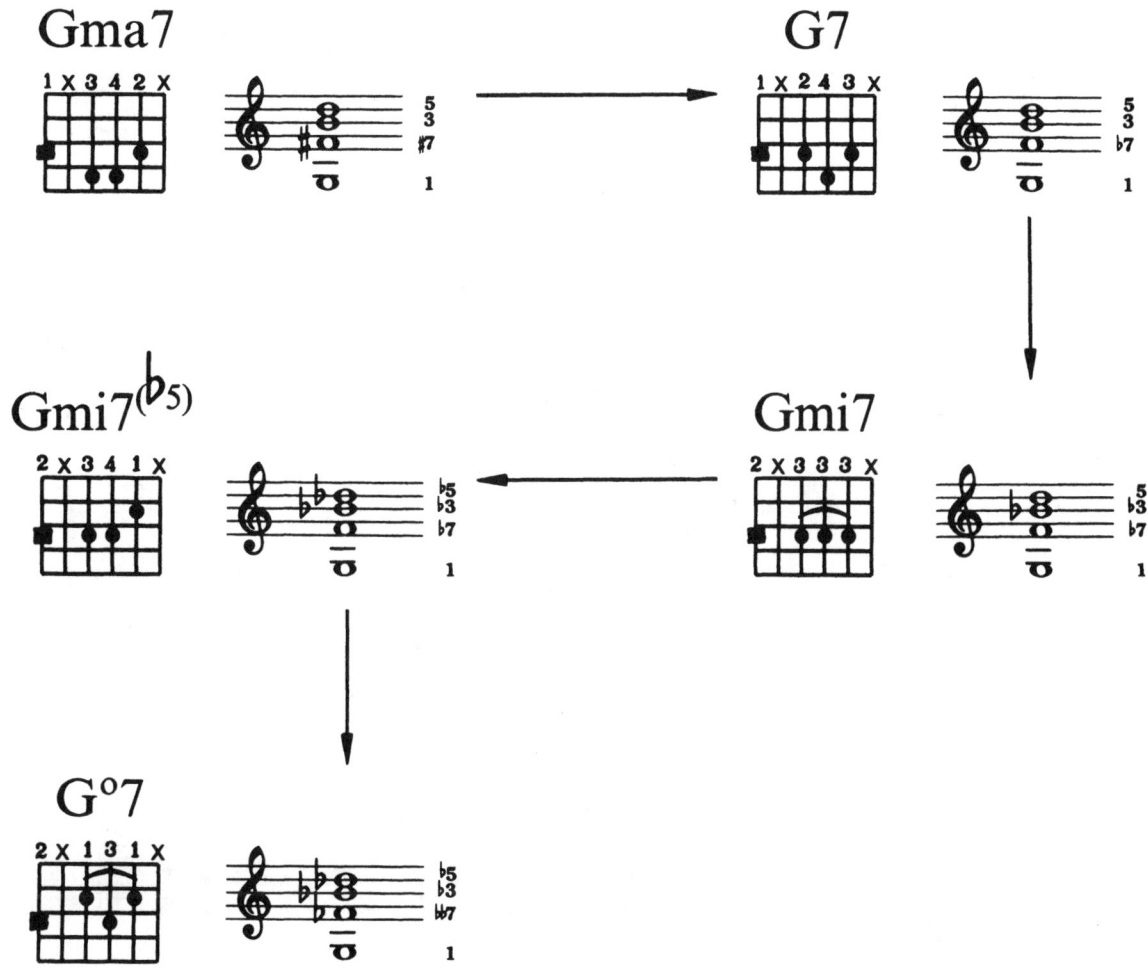

Now play the series backwards from G07 to GMA7.

Ex. 59

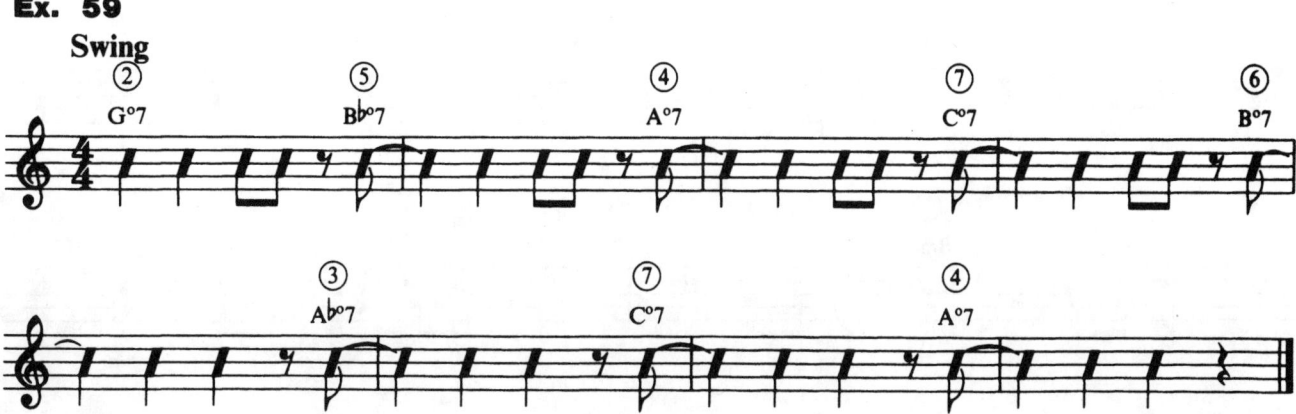

REVIEW
Review of diminished chords and other chords.

Ex. 60

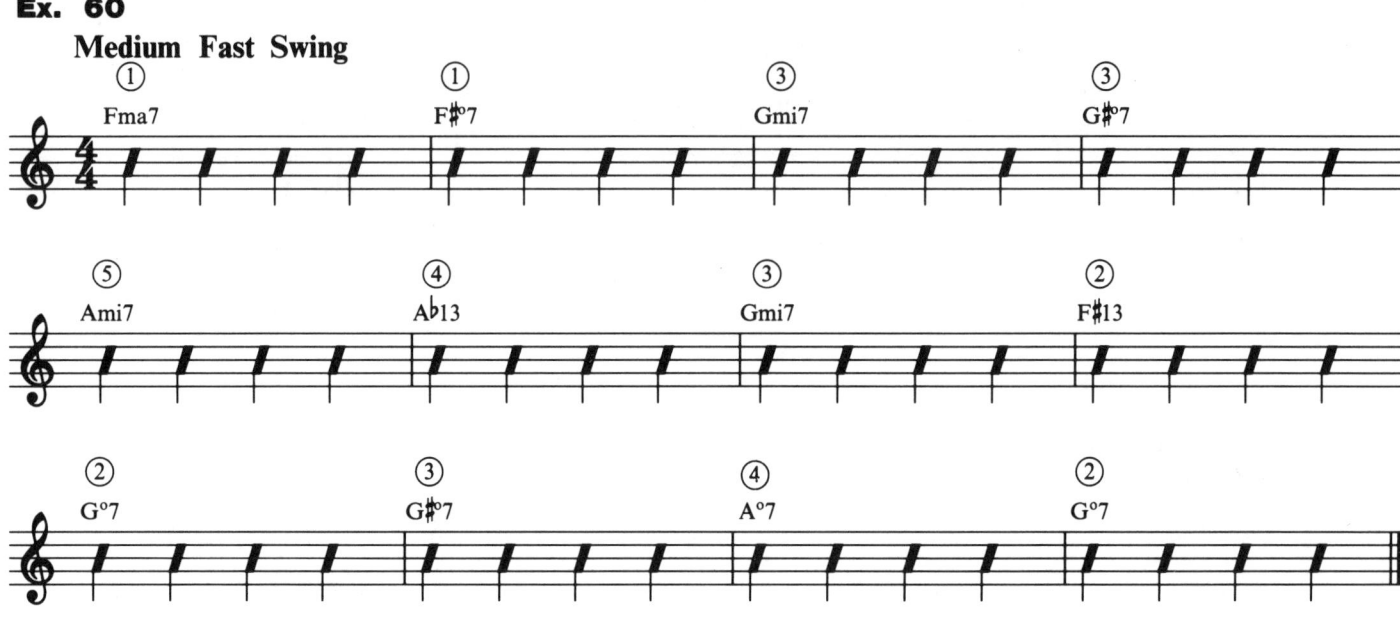

A Bossa with accents on two and four.

Ex. 61

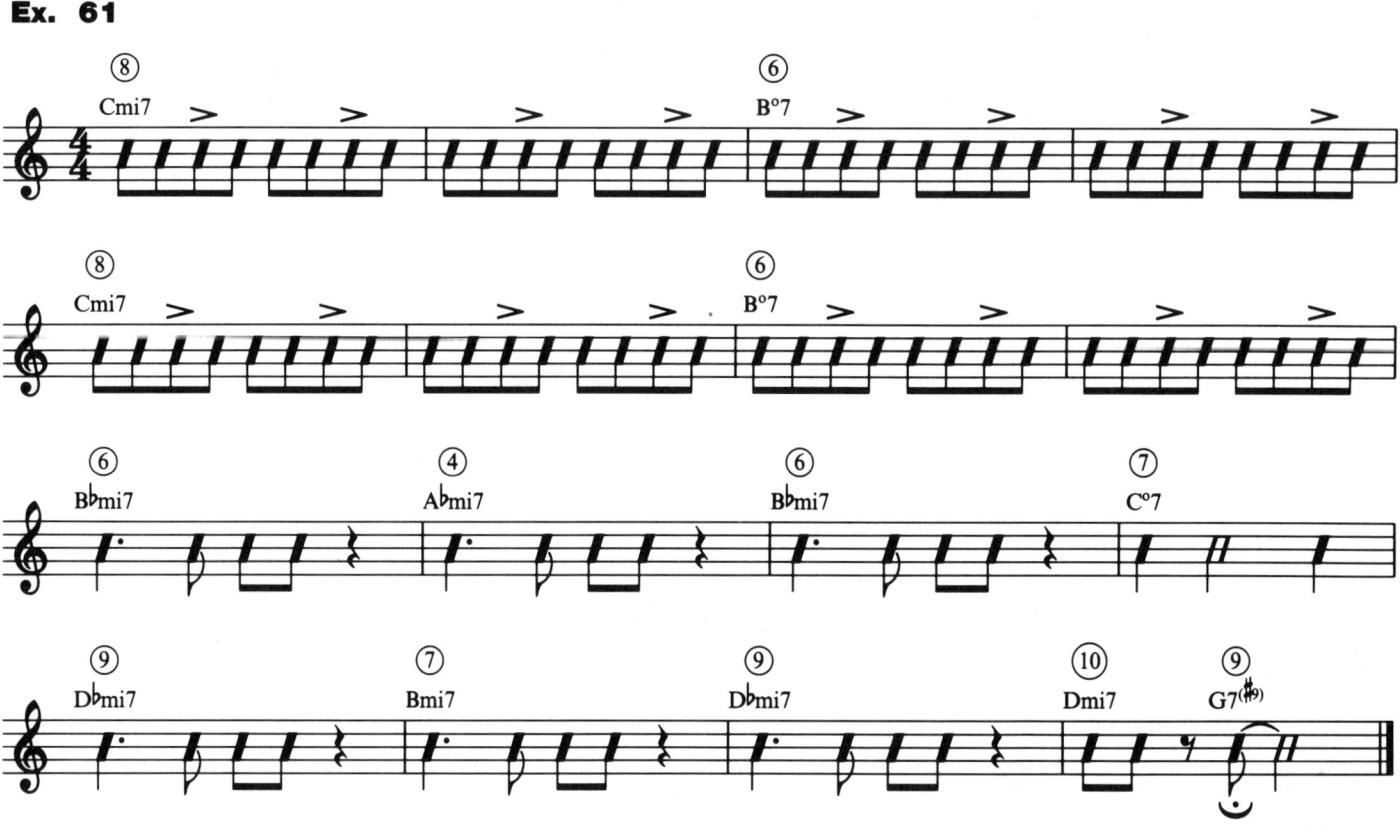

BAR CHORDS: EARLY ROCK RHYTHM STYLE

These are very important guitar chords because of their unique sound and mobility. There are no open strings within the chord and bar chords can be moved all over the neck with ease. Rock players use bar chords often because of their powerful sound. The top chord in each column is the basic triad on which the chords beneath are based. There are no alterations in bar chords. Many of the notes in the chord are doubled and tripled.

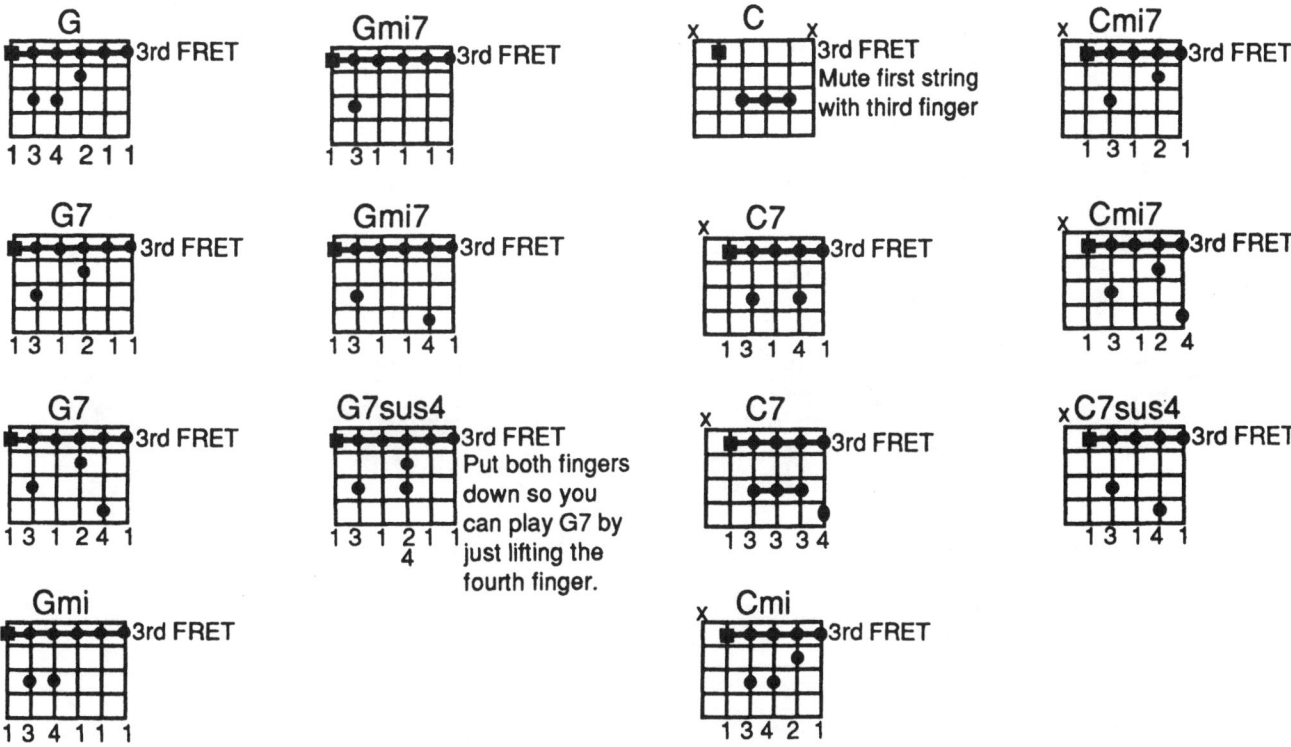

If your are having trouble with some of the bar chords, experiment moving your left arm to the left or closer or further from your body. This changes the angle your fingers hit the strings.

Practice the two main voicings:

Use the middle pick up position. Practice both forms of the seventh on page 65. Listen to the different sound of each. In this early Rock ballad style, use all down strokes and accent two and four.

Ex. 62

50's Rock

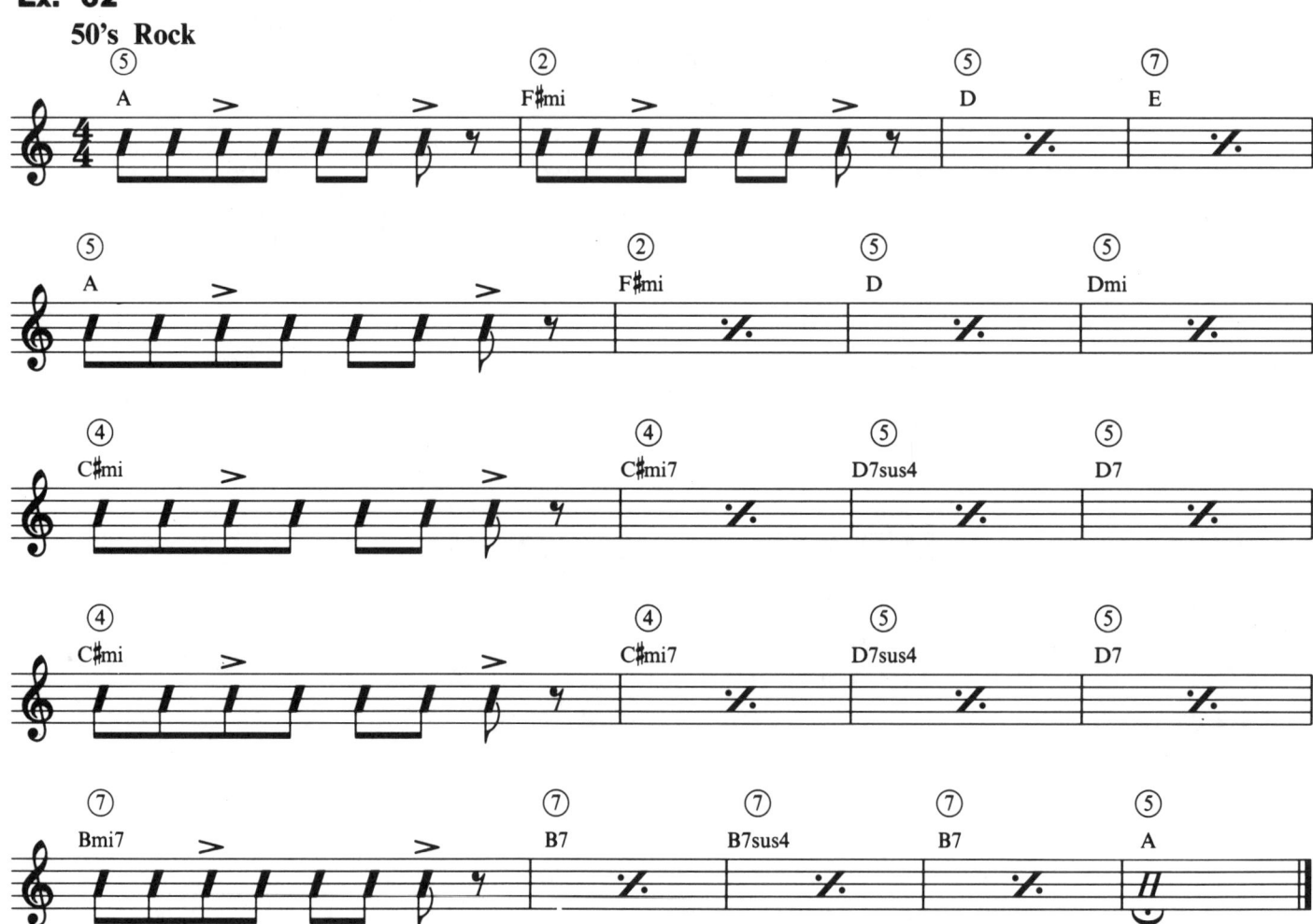

THE "POWER CHORD" HEAVY METAL STYLE

This chord is an outgrowth of the bar chord. The power chord has only two pitches, the root and fifth. Since this chord has no third, it is neither major or minor. Power chords are usually used in a Rock setting. To get the right sound, you'll need some distortion on your amp. Here are some ways to achieve this effect. There might be a distortion switch or control on the amp. If not, turn the master volume to 0, turn the volume to 10, and turn the master volume back up to desired playing volume. If none of the above are possible with your amp, get a distortion pedal. Plug the guitar into the pedal, then the pedal into the amp. Use the bridge pickup. When playing this style, slide from one chord to the next when playing on the same strings.

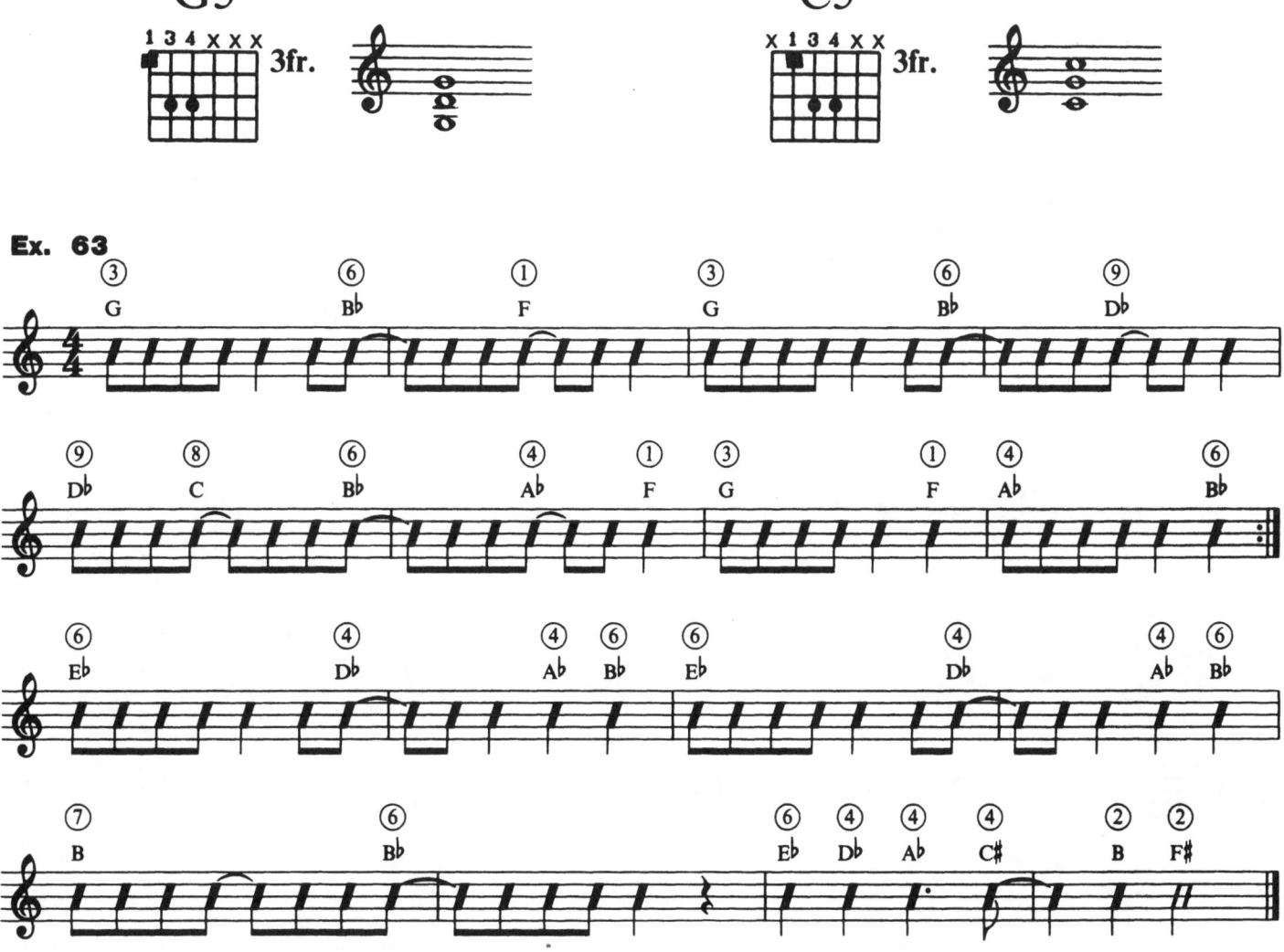

THE "CHUCK BERRY" EARLY ROCK STYLE

If the arranger wants this type of rhythm, it will probably be written as just four slash marks with the words "Chuck Berry" at the beginning:

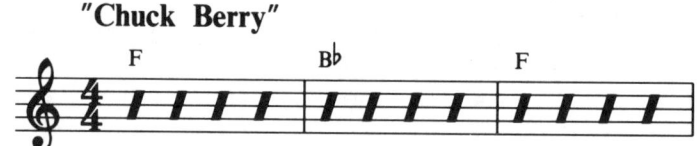

You should start with a power chord and move the fifth up to the sixth and back down as shown below.

Use middle or bridge pickup position and very slight distortion on the amp to simulate the early tube amps.

Use all down strokes.

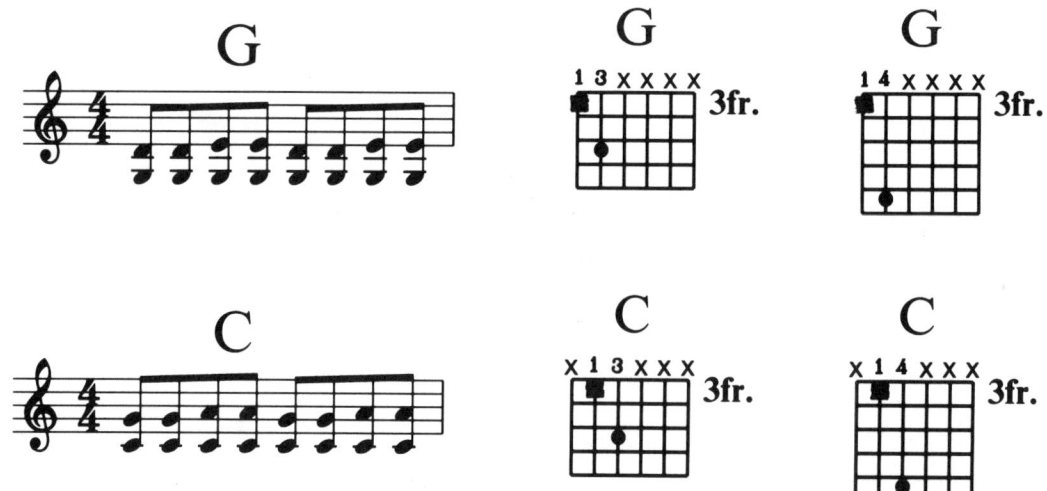

Ex. 64

50's Rock

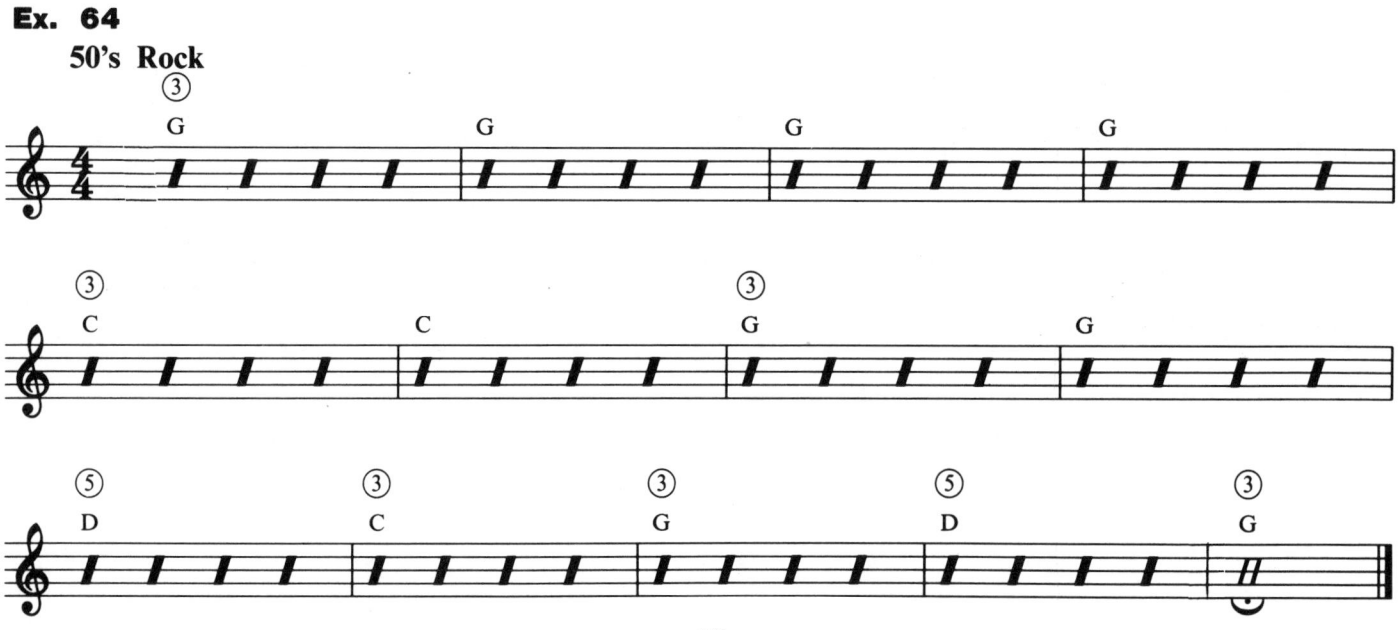

This is a variation on the rhythm on page 68. After moving the fifth in the chord up to the sixth, it moves up again to the lowered seventh.

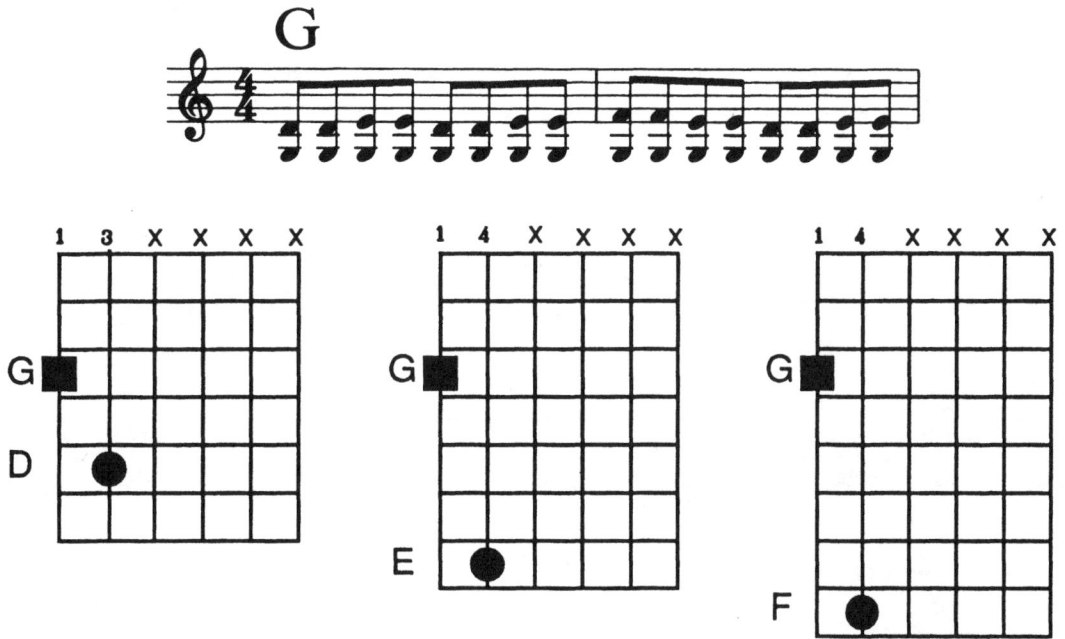

Play these changes using the rhythm variation. This is a two measure pattern, so when the chord lasts one measure, use just the first half of the pattern.

Ex. 65

50's Rock

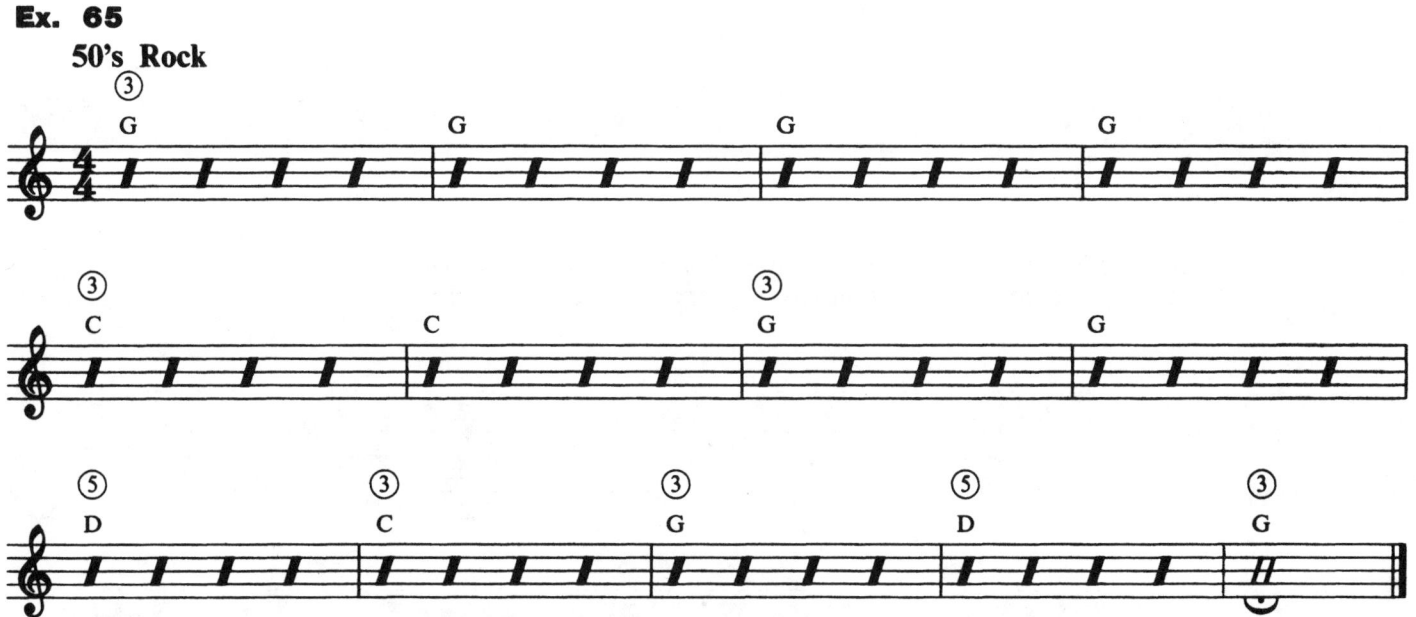

Another variation is a rhythmic change on the same notes. Dotted rhythms are used to create a shuffle feel. Example 66 uses the same chords as Example 65. Change the rhythm to dotted eighth-sixteenth to play this shuffle groove.

SIXTEENTH NOTE "FUNK RHYTHMS"

The sixteenth note gets 1/4 beat. There are four sixteenth notes in one beat. Most Rock and Funk music has syncopated rhythms made up of sixteenth notes and other note values. To help you get into these rhythms, we'll start with a tapping exercise, which contains quarters, eighths, and sixteenths.

Tap along with the tape.

Ex. 67

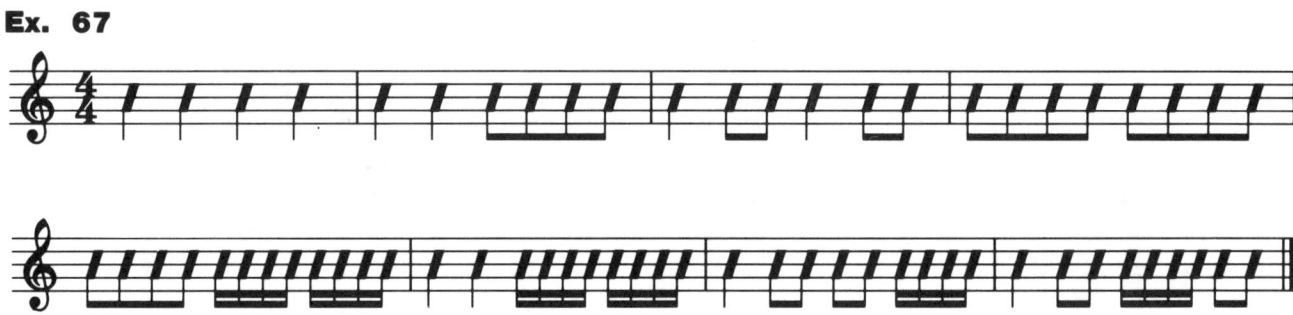

The beat can also be divided into eighth and sixteenth combinations.

Ex. 68

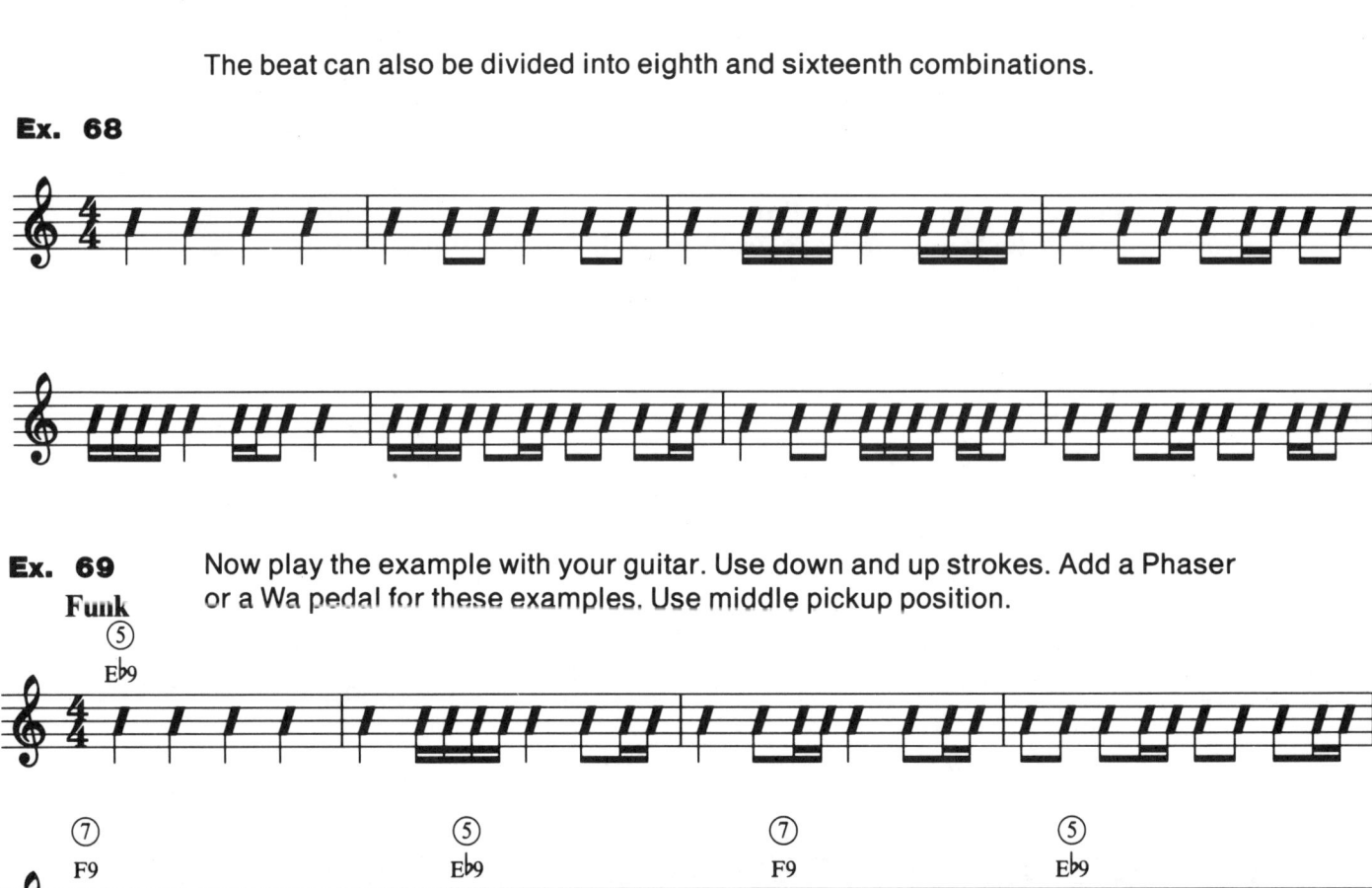

Ex. 69
Funk

Now play the example with your guitar. Use down and up strokes. Add a Phaser or a Wa pedal for these examples. Use middle pickup position.

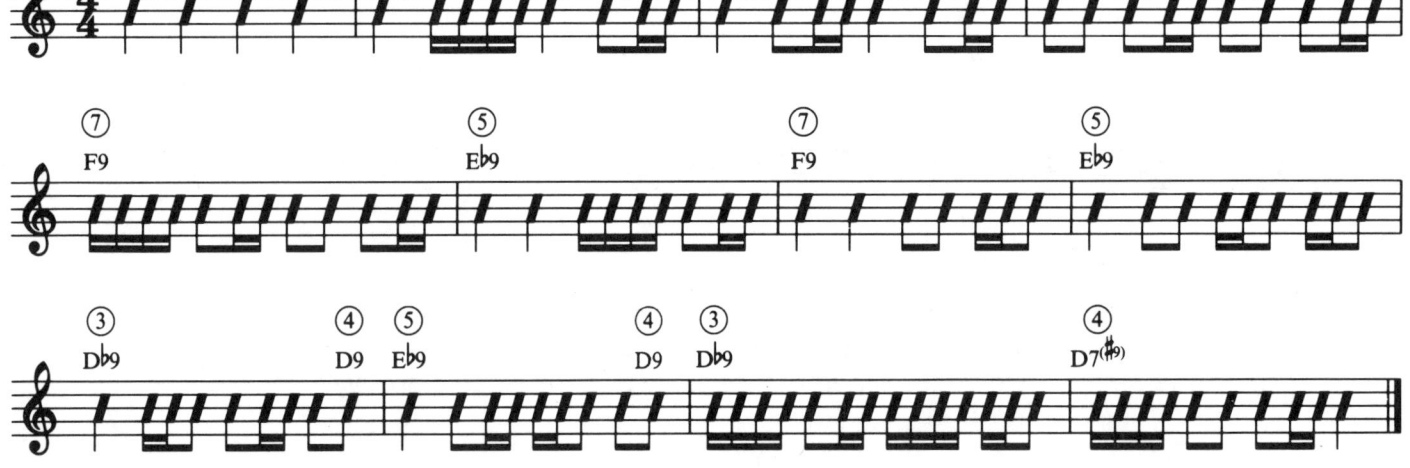

Ex. 70

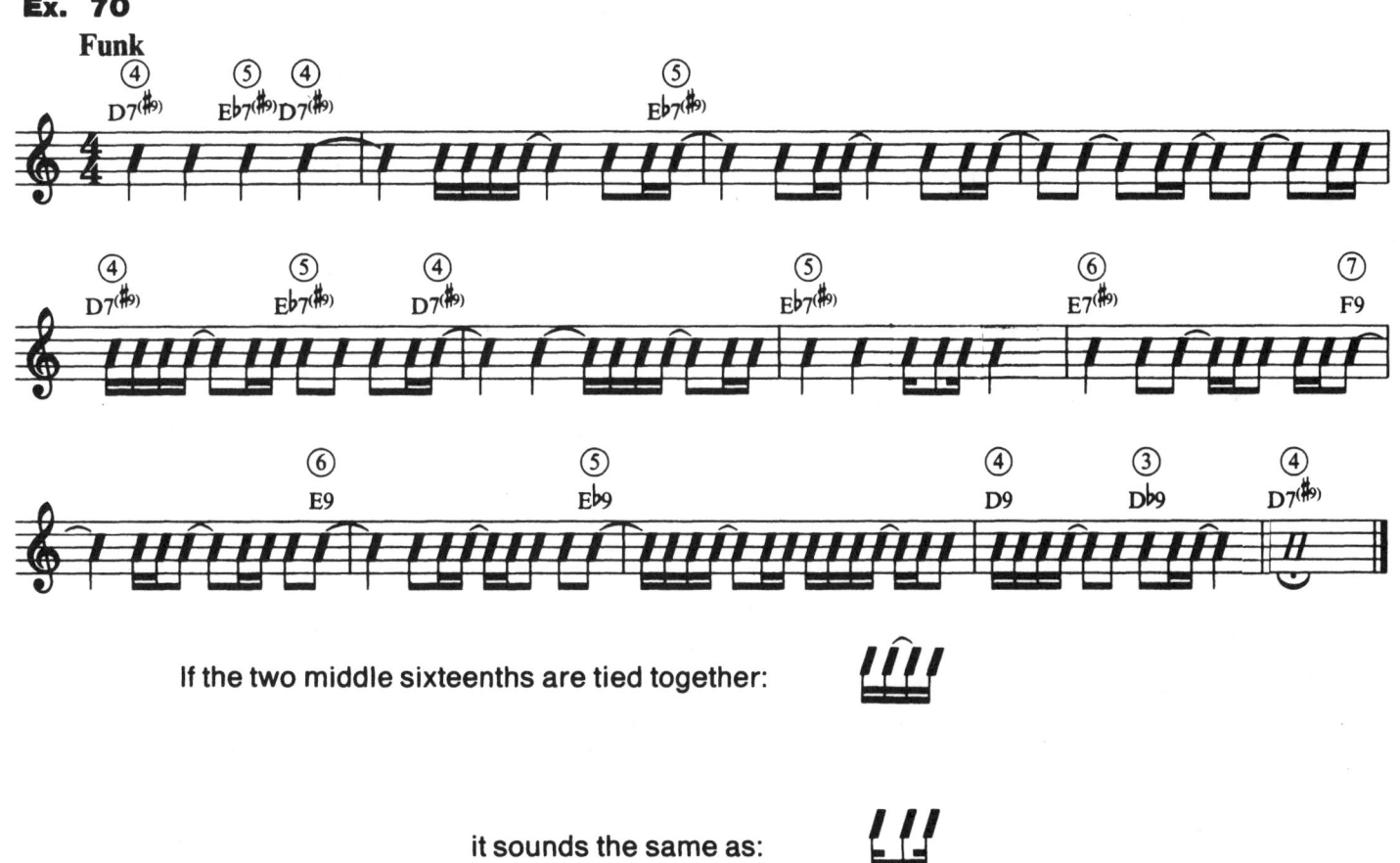

If the two middle sixteenths are tied together:

it sounds the same as:

This exercise uses the same eighth and sixteenth patterns as Example 68. Some ties are added to emphasize the syncopations.

Ex. 71

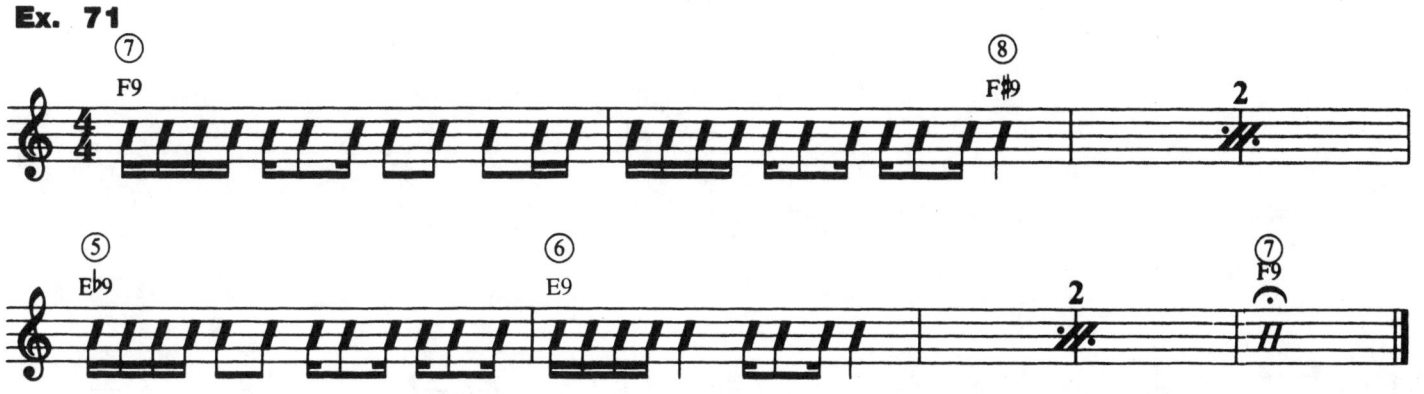

One or more sixteenths may be removed and replaced with a rest. Tap along with the tape.

Ex. 72

SIXTEENTH NOTE STRUMMING WITH MUTED, PERCUSSIVE SOUNDS

In certain funk music a wa wa pedal is used which brings out an interesting sound when the chords are muted. Release the pressure on the strings, but leave your fingers in place as in the Samba. The wa should start the measure with the toe up. Smoothly go down on 1, up on 2, down on 3, up on 4, while strumming even sixteenth notes. When you understand the process, make up your own patterns and vary them during the piece.

Ex. 73

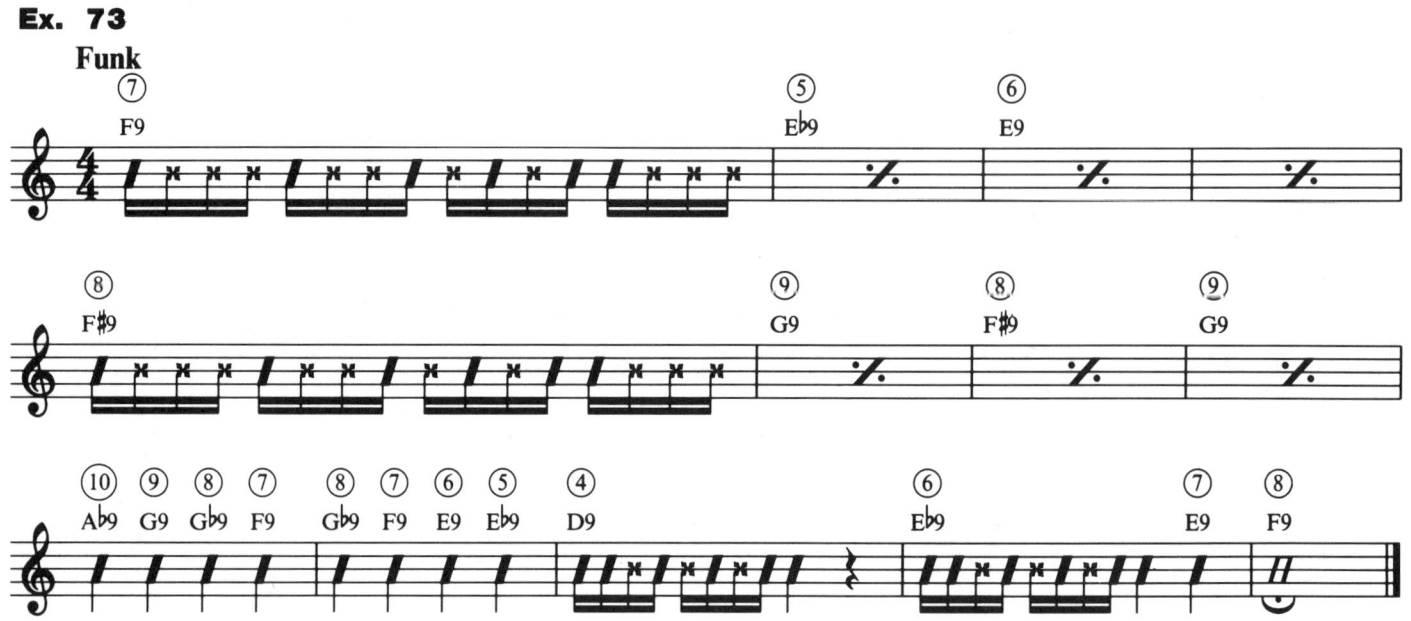

REGGAE

The guitarist plays a very important role in this music. Play just "back beats," a chord on the second and fourth beats with an up stroke. The chord is released shortly after striking so that it is short. Use bar chords.

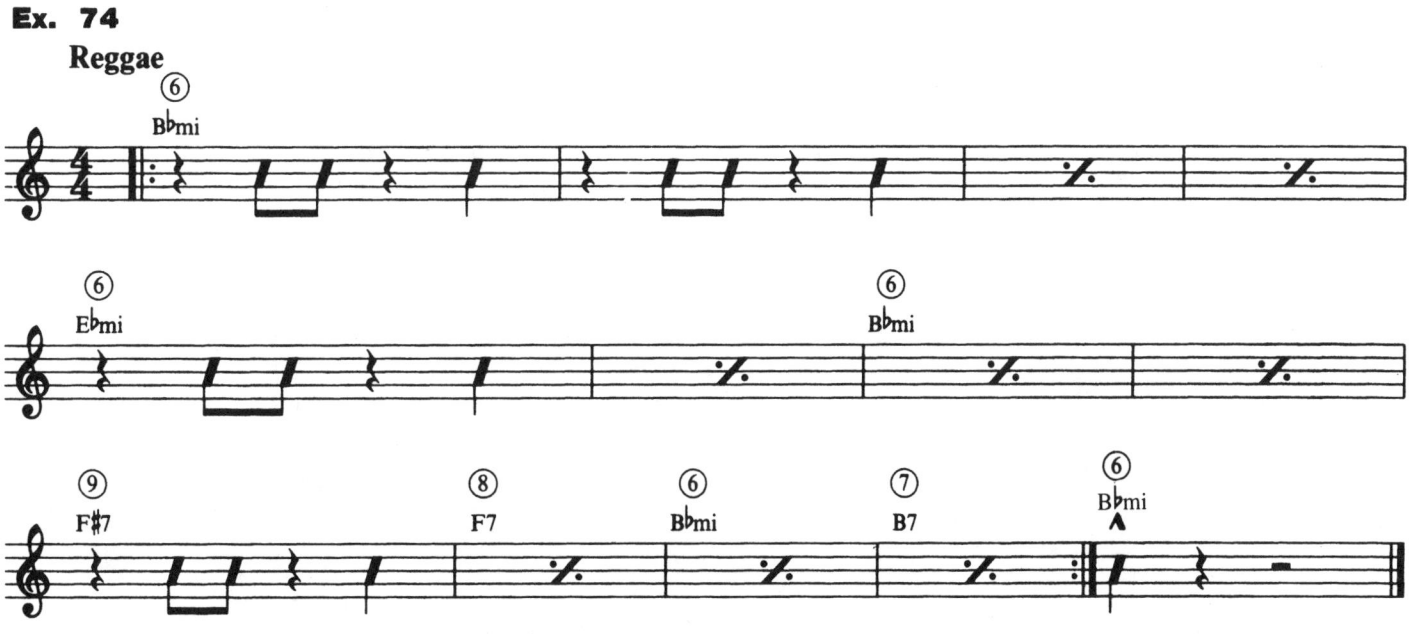

Ex. 74

TRIADS WITH ALTERED ROOTS (SLASH CHORDS)

This type of chord tells you what the bass player is playing under the chord. It can be either a note that is not usually in the chord or a note that is in the chord other than the root. If possible, you should play the chord with the bass note on the bottom of the chord. It doubles the note the bass player is playing and enhances the harmonic effect. Sometimes these are impossible to play on guitar. In that case, just ignore the note on the right of the slash and play the chord to the left.

There are three ways of making a triad using strings 2,3,4. The bass note is played on the sixth string. Try using a pick on the bass note while picking the triad with fingers.

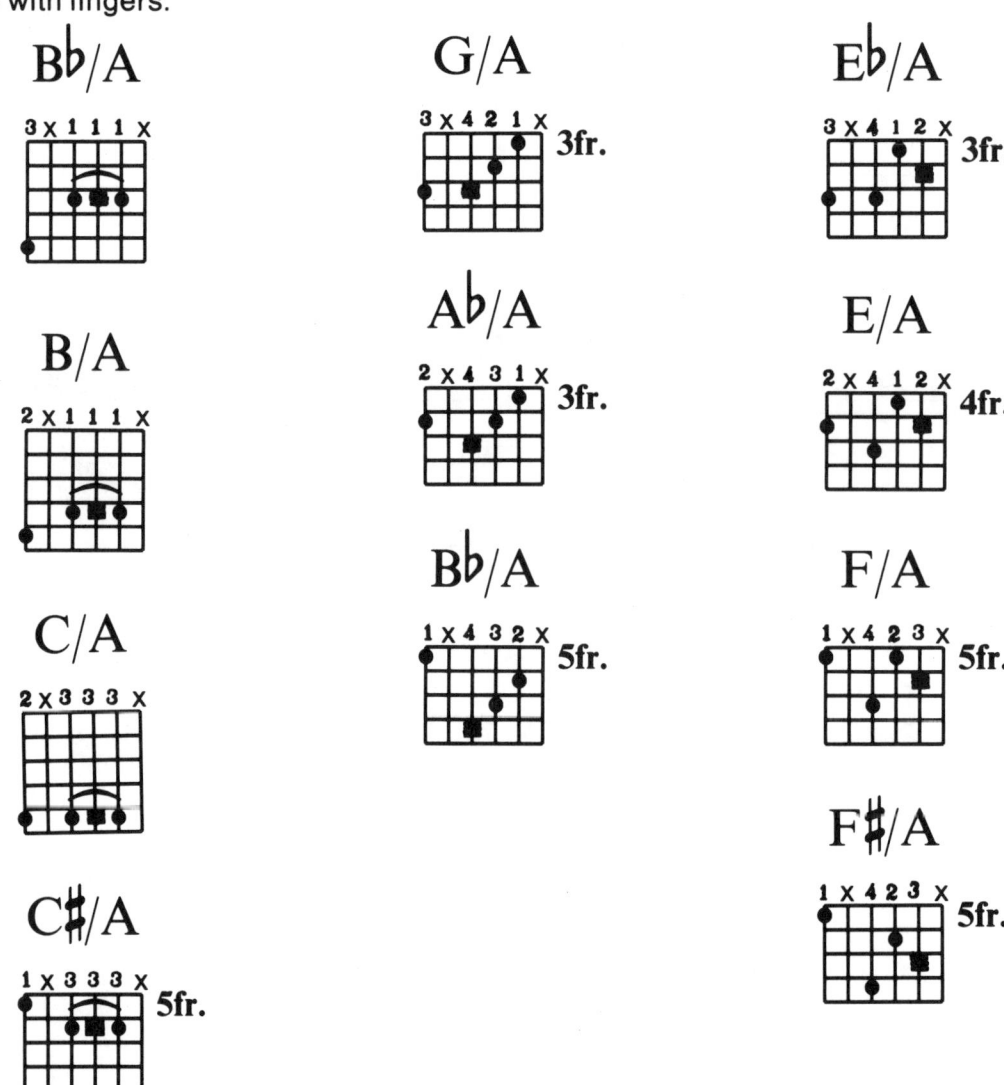

RESPONDING TO DRUM FILLS, HORN FIGURES AND PIANO PLAYERS

1. DRUM FILLS - Usually the guitar part does not have the drum fills marked. You should make a mental note where these are or mark them on the chart in pencil. The drum fill is usually improvised, and a good drummer will play a different fill each time. It can be better to play a long chord or nothing at all during a drum fill than to play a contrasting rhythm. Also, make note of where the drummer comes out of the fill, so you can accent that beat.

2. HORN FIGURES - Since most of the guitar charts that you play contain just four slash marks per measure, your job should be to improve on the music by rhythmically fitting in to what's happening. Sometimes four quarter notes are a direct contradiction to the rhythm the horns are playing. Again, make note of where these clashes occur. Professional guitar players write the horn rhythms on the charts so the chords will fit better. Always play the correct volume. Get louder or softer with the band. It may seem like you are unimportant, but if you pay attention to these details you can be a team player and improve your bands' sound.

3. PIANO PLAYERS - The key to the success of your rhythm section is listening! You and the piano player must work together. Here are a few ideas to get started.

    A. Talk with your director about trading comping duties behind soloists. For example: the piano could comp behind the trumpet solo and the guitar behind the tenor solo, etc.

    B. Use this same concept when playing behind ensemble passages. You don't both have to play all the time. Experiment and ask your director what sounds the best.

    C. Practice playing rhythmic fills exactly together.

    D. Practice playing complimentary styles. That is, the guitar could play a whole note on each chord change, and the piano could play a more rhythmically active part. Or, the two of you can comp and fill around each other and the band.

    E. Many contemporary tunes have vital guitar and piano parts which are both needed to make the chart work. For these you should play your part exactly as written.

Well, that's it. The book is finished. I hope you learned something to improve your playing with the jazz ensemble. If you can play everything in the book now, I recommend putting on the tape and playing every example without stopping. Do this occasionally as a review and to keep your chording and reading "chops" up.

Music is not played by your guitar or your amp. It is played by you. The famous piano artist Cecil Taylor said, "Music is everything you do." The type of person you are comes out in your music. So, in addition to learning the technical art of playing an instrument, you must also work on improving the human instrument to achieve the best music.

PLAY LIKE THE PROS

Jazz Guitar Instruction & Transcriptions from Hal Leonard

The Jazz Style of Tal Farlow
THE ELEMENTS OF BEBOP GUITAR
by Steve Rochinski
Finally, the book that defines the melodic and harmonic thinking behind the style of one of the most influential jazz guitarists of the 20th century, Tal Farlow. Includes instruction on: creating single-line solos; visualizing the neck; use of anticipation, expansion, and contraction; reharmonization; signature and chord voicings; chord-melody concepts; special signature effects such as bongos and harmonics; tune and solo transcriptions; and more!
00673245..$19.95

50 Essential Bebop Heads Arranged for Guitar
The best lines of Charlie Parker, Dizzy Gillespie, Thelonius Monk, and many more, for guitar with notes and tab. Includes: Donna Lee • Groovin' High • Ornithology • Confirmation • Epistrophy • and more.
00698990..$14.95

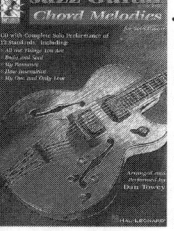

Jazz Guitar Chord Melodies
FOR SOLO GUITAR
arranged & performed by Dan Towey
This book/CD pack offers performance level chord-melody arrangements of 12 popular jazz songs for the solo guitarist. They range in difficulty from intermediate to advanced and include notes and tab. The CD includes complete solo performances. Songs include: All the Things You Are • Body and Soul • My Romance • How Insensitive • My One and Only Love • and more.
00698988 Book/CD Pack..$19.95

Chord Melody Standards for Guitar
15 great songs, including: Autumn in New York • Cheek to Cheek • Easy Living • Georgia on My Mind • The Girl from Ipanema • Have You Met Miss Jones? • Isn't It Romantic? • Stella by Starlight • The Way You Look Tonight • When I Fall in Love • When Sunny Gets Blue • more.
00699128..$9.95

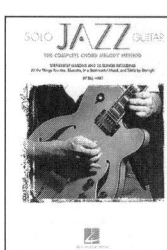

Solo Jazz Guitar
The book starts with 11 lessons on chord melody concepts, then uses 20 familiar jazz standards to demonstrate these techniques, covering: diatonic and minor third substitution, contrary motion, back cycles, walking bass lines, modal chord scales, and more. Songs (in standard notation & TAB) include: All the Things You Are • Cherokee • Giant Steps • I Could Write a Book • Like Someone in Love • My Romance • Yesterdays • more.
00695317..$9.95

Best of Jazz Guitar
by Wolf Marshall
Signature Licks
Wolf Marshall provides a hands-on analysis of 10 of the most frequently played tunes in the jazz genre, as played by the leading guitarists of all time. Features: "St. Thomas" performed by Jim Hall, Tal Farlow and Kenny Burrell • "All Blues" performed by George Benson, Kenny Burrell and Pat Martino • "Satin Doll" performed by Howard Roberts and Joe Pass • "I'll Remember April" performed by Johnny Smith and Grant Green • and more!
00695586 Book/CD Pack..$24.95

101 Must-Know Jazz Licks
by Wolf Marshall
Signature Licks
Now you can add authentic jazz feel and flavor to your playing! Here are 101 definitive licks, plus a demonstration CD, from every major jazz guitar style, neatly organized into easy-to-use categories. They're all here: swing and pre-bop, bebop, post-bop modern jazz, hard bop and cool jazz, modal jazz, soul jazz and postmodern jazz. Includes an introduction by Wolf Marshall, tips for using the book and CD, and a listing of suggested recordings.
00695433 Book/CD Pack..$14.95

Jazz Guitar Improvisation
by Sid Jacobs
Develop your solo skills with this comprehensive method which includes a CD with 99 full demonstration tracks. Topics covered include: common jazz phrases; applying scales and arpeggios; guide tones, non-chordal tones, fourths; and more. Includes standard notation and tablature.
00695128 Book/CD Pack..$17.95

Joe Pass Collection
12 songs transcribed, including: Blues for Basie • Blues for Hank • Cheek to Cheek • Dissonance #1 • Happy Holiday Blues • I Got Rhythm • In a Sentimental Mood • Pasta Blues • Satin Doll • The Song Is You • The Way You Look Tonight • Yardbird Suite.
00672353..$16.95

JAZZ GUITAR GREATS

Learn the best lines of the masters! Each book/CD pack includes note-for-note legendary jazz performances transcribed and performed by Jack Grassel. The CD features two versions of each song at different tempos, with the rhythm section on a different channel. Includes standard notation and tablature.

Jazz Guitar Classics
Includes: Satin Doll/Kenny Burrell • Tangerine/Jimmy Raney • Honeysuckle Rose/Django Reinhardt • Billie's Bounce/George Benson • Stella by Starlight/Tal Farlow • Easy Living/Johnny Smith.
00698998 Book/CD Pack..$19.95

Jazz Guitar Favorites
Includes: All the Things That You Are/Hank Garland • I Hear a Symphony/Howard Roberts • Oleo/Pat Martino • Speak Low/Barney Kessel • When Sunny Gets Blue/George Barnes • Yesterdays/Wes Montgomery.
00698999 Book/CD Pack..$19.95

Jazz Guitar Standards
Includes: Falling in Love With You/Grant Green • I've Got You Under My Skin/Jim Hall • A Night in Tunisia/Billy Bauer • Stompin' at the Savoy/Charlie Christian • Yardbird Suite/Joe Pass • You Brought a New Kind of Love to Me/Chuck Wayne.
00672356 Book/CD Pack..$19.95

FOR MORE INFORMATION, SEE YOUR LOCAL MUSIC DEALER, OR WRITE TO:

HAL•LEONARD® CORPORATION
7777 W. BLUEMOUND RD. P.O. BOX 13819 MILWAUKEE, WI 53213
www.halleonard.com

Prices, contents and availability subject to change without notice.

0301

ARTIST TRANSCRIPTIONS

Artist Transcriptions are authentic, note-for-note transcriptions of the hottest artists in jazz, pop, and rock today. These outstanding, accurate arrangements are in an easy-to-read format which includes all essential lines. Artist Transcriptions can be used to perform, sequence or reference.

GUITAR & BASS

The Guitar Book of Pierre Bensusan
00699072.................................$19.95

Ron Carter – Acoustic Bass
00672331.................................$16.95

**Charley Christian –
The Art of Jazz Guitar**
00026704.................................$8.95

Stanley Clarke Collection
00672307.................................$19.95

Al Di Meola – Cielo E Terra
00604041.................................$14.95

**Al Di Meola –
Friday Night in San Francisco**
00660115.................................$14.95

Al Di Meola – Music, Words, Pictures
00604043.................................$14.95

Kevin Eubanks Guitar Collection
00672319.................................$19.95

The Jazz Style of Tal Farlow
00673245.................................$19.95

Bela Fleck and the Flecktones
00672359 Melody/Lyrics/Chords....$14.95

David Friesen – Departure
00673221.................................$14.95

David Friesen – Years Through Time
00673253.................................$14.95

Best Of Frank Gambale
00672336.................................$22.95

Jim Hall – Jazz Guitar Environments
00699389 Book/CD........................$19.95

Jim Hall – Exploring Jazz Guitar
00699306.................................$16.95

Scott Henderson Guitar Book
00699330.................................$19.95

**Allan Holdsworth –
Reaching for the Uncommon Chord**
00604049.................................$14.95

Leo Kottke – Eight Songs
00699215.................................$14.95

Wes Montgomery – Guitar Transcriptions
00675536.................................$14.95

Joe Pass Collection
00672353.................................$16.95

John Patitucci
00673216.................................$14.95

Django Reinhardt Anthology
00027083.................................$14.95

The Genius of Django Reinhardt
00026711.................................$10.95

Django Reinhardt – A Treasury of Songs
00026715.................................$12.95

**John Renbourn – The Nine Maidens,
The Hermit, Stefan and John**
00699071.................................$12.95

Great Rockabilly Guitar Solos
00692820.................................$14.95

John Scofield – Guitar Transcriptions
00603390.................................$16.95

**Andres Segovia –
20 Studies for the Guitar**
00006362 Book/Cassette.............$14.95

Johnny Smith Guitar Solos
00672374.................................$14.95

Mike Stern Guitar Book
00673224.................................$16.95

Mark Whitfield
00672320.................................$19.95

Jack Wilkins – Windows
00673249.................................$14.95

Gary Willis Collection
00672337.................................$19.95

CLARINET

Buddy De Franco Collection
00672423.................................$19.95

FLUTE

James Newton – Improvising Flute
00660108.................................$14.95

The Lew Tabackin Collection
00672455.................................$19.95

TROMBONE

J.J. Johnson Collection
00672332.................................$19.95

TRUMPET

Randy Brecker
00673234.................................$14.95

**The Brecker Brothers...
And All Their Jazz**
00672351.................................$19.95

Best of the Brecker Brothers
00672447.................................$19.95

Miles Davis – Standards
00672450.................................$19.95

Freddie Hubbard
00673214.................................$14.95

Tom Harrell Jazz Trumpet
00672382.................................$19.95

Jazz Trumpet Solos
00672363.................................$9.95

PIANO & KEYBOARD

Monty Alexander Collection
00672338.................................$19.95

Kenny Barron Collection
00672318.................................$22.95

Warren Bernhardt Collection
00672364.................................$19.95

Cyrus Chesnut Collection
00672437.................................$19.95

Billy Childs Collection
00673242.................................$19.95

Chick Corea – Elektric Band
00603126.................................$15.95

Chick Corea – Paint the World
00672300.................................$12.95

Bill Evans Collection
00672365.................................$19.95

Benny Green Collection
00672329.................................$19.95

Herbie Hancock Collection
00672419.................................$19.95

Gene Harris Collection
00672446.................................$19.95

Ahmad Jamal Collection
00672322.................................$22.95

Jazz Master Classics for Piano
00672354.................................$14.95

**Thelonious Monk – Intermediate
Piano Solos**
00672392.................................$12.95

Jelly Roll Morton – The Piano Rolls
00672433.................................$12.95

Michel Petrucciani
00673226.................................$17.95

Bud Powell Classics
00672371.................................$19.95

André Previn Collection
00672437.................................$19.95

Horace Silver Collection
00672303.................................$19.95

Art Tatum Collection
00672316.................................$22.95

Art Tatum Solo Book
00672355.................................$19.95

Billy Taylor Collection
00672357.................................$24.95

McCoy Tyner
00673215.................................$14.95

Cedar Walton Collection
00672321.................................$19.95

SAXOPHONE

Julian "Cannonball" Adderly Collection
00673244.................................$16.95

Michael Brecker
00673237.................................$18.95

Michael Brecker Collection
00672429.................................$17.95

**The Brecker Brothers...
And All Their Jazz**
00672351.................................$19.95

Best of the Brecker Brothers
00672447.................................$19.95

Benny Carter Plays Standards
00672315.................................$22.95

Benny Carter Collection
00672314.................................$22.95

James Carter Collection
00672394.................................$19.95

John Coltrane – Giant Steps
00672349.................................$19.95

John Coltrane Solos
00673233.................................$22.95

Paul Desmond Collection
00672328.................................$19.95

Paul Desmond Plays Standards
00672454.................................$19.95

Stan Getz
00699375.................................$16.95

Stan Getz – Bossa Novas
00672377.................................$17.95

Great Tenor Sax Solos
00673254.................................$18.95

**Joe Henderson – Selections from
"Lush Life" & "So Near So Far"**
00673252.................................$19.95

Best of Joe Henderson
00672330.................................$22.95

Jazz Master Classics for Tenor Sax
00672350.................................$18.95

Best Of Kenny G
00673239.................................$19.95

Kenny G – Breathless
00673229.................................$19.95

Kenny G – Classics in the Key of G
00672462.................................$19.95

Kenny G – The Moment
00672373.................................$19.95

Joe Lovano Collection
00672326.................................$19.95

James Moody Collection – Sax and Flute
00672372.................................$19.95

The Frank Morgan Collection
00672416.................................$19.95

The Art Pepper Collection
00672301.................................$19.95

Sonny Rollins Collection
00672444.................................$19.95

David Sanborn Collection
00675000.................................$14.95

The Lew Tabackin Collection
00672455.................................$19.95

Stanley Turrentine Collection
00672334.................................$19.95

Ernie Watts Saxophone Collection
00673256.................................$18.95

FOR MORE INFORMATION, SEE YOUR LOCAL MUSIC DEALER, OR WRITE TO:

HAL•LEONARD® CORPORATION
7777 W. BLUEMOUND RD. P.O. BOX 13819 MILWAUKEE, WI 53213

Visit our web site for a complete listing of our titles with songlists.
www.halleonard.com

Prices and availability subject to change without notice.
Some products may not be available outside the U.S.A.